WHY ROME

WHY
ROME

By

SELDEN PEABODY DELANY

LINCOLN MAC VEAGH
THE DIAL PRESS
NEW YORK · MCMXXX
LONGMANS, GREEN & CO., TORONTO

MANUFACTURED IN THE UNITED STATES OF AMERICA
BY THE VAIL-BALLOU PRESS, INC., BINGHAMTON, N. Y.

TABLE OF CONTENTS

PREFACE

Life is a pilgrimage, and the goal of our pilgrimage is God. Nothing else really matters: our work, financial status, worldly success, social standing, pleasures, sufferings. We are pilgrims of eternity. Our unaided reason cannot fully tell us whence we came, or why we are here. Our faces are set towards the vast open spaces that are shrouded in mystery. We are looking for a guide who can direct us to the right path, that we may not lose our way. We cannot give up our quest, and simply settle down and be comfortable in our present surroundings. We must somehow get on the track of Him who is responsible for our being here, and who alone can enlighten us about the meaning of life and the purpose of the universe.

Nothing is more interesting about a man than his search for God. It is nothing to be ashamed of. We delight in reading books of travel and adventure, the life-stories of those who have made decisive scientific discoveries, and the autobiographies of men of action or men of thought. If more men and women would honestly reveal to us the spiritual ad-

ventures which have come to them in their attempt
to find God and ascertain his will for them, they
would bequeath to their fellows human documents
of real value.

For this reason I make no apology for the personal element that enters so frequently into this
narrative. However commonplace my own spiritual
adventure may appear from my account of it, to
me it has been of absorbing interest. Unfortunately,
while we are still living and working in a world
where human relationships play so important a part,
the personal element cannot be given the space it
deserves.

In a pilgrimage one does not stand still. The life
of a pilgrim is one of ceaseless changes—change of
scenery, companions, horizons, inner experiences of
mind and soul. I have no feeling of envy toward
people whose lives are uneventful and changeless.
They miss a lot of fun. The inhabitants of our cem-
eteries change least of all. In my own chameleon-
like transformations, I have been comforted by the
words of Cardinal Newman in his *Essay on the
Development of Christian Doctrine:* "In a higher
world it is otherwise, but here below to live is to
change, and to be perfect is to have changed often."

A pilgrimage, however, is not a perfect metaphor
to describe the search for God. It implies a roaming

about the world, in the hope that somewhere, in some promised land, God will suddenly appear in all his glory. We shall never find God unless we seek Him in our own souls. Here we have the authority of St. Augustine to reassure us: "I sought Thee and I found Thee not, because I sought Thee without. Again I sought Thee and found Thee, because I sought in my own soul."

One reason why so few people find God today is that most of us never take time to be alone. We are always on the lookout for somebody who will rescue us from the dire calamity of spending an evening alone. We dine with the crowd, we seek our amusements with the crowd, we even try to pray with the crowd. If we do succeed in escaping, our solitude is invaded by the telephone and the radio. We let it be invaded. What is the explanation of this almost universal fear of being alone? I suspect it is largely that we are running away from God. It is a terrifying experience to be alone with one's conscience, when one may often hear the voice of God tolling like a great bell—and as ceaselessly. We know then that we cannot do the thing that we want to do, but that we must do something else that goes against all our inclinations.

It was when alone in Europe last summer that I had a spiritual experience of God which shook my life to its foundations. It brought me face to face with reality, and I knew that I could no longer pursue the course which I had presumptuously mapped out for myself. Since then I have been trying to escape from the insistent demands of God, but could not. Through it all, I have learned the truth of the saying that, "we are never less alone than when alone." When we are "alone with the Alone" we become conscious of our vocation; and woe to the man who tries to run away!

There is nothing funnier than a man who is trying to escape from God. I am not one of those who think there is no place for humor in religion. One of my chief objections to much that passes for Christianity in America is that it is totally lacking in a sense of humor. It is too long-faced and solemn and lugubrious. One of the marks of the true Church—as it has always been a mark of the saints —is the note of joy and mirthfulness. If we become too serious about our religion, we shall be in danger of losing it entirely. I warn my readers not to read even this book in too serious a frame of mind. I warn them also that it is not a scholarly theological treatise. It is merely a collection of chapters from the diary of a pilgrimage.

Much as I should like to talk personally with all the friends and parishioners who have for years been under my spiritual guidance, I know that is impossible. Yet I feel that I owe them some explanation of the transfer of my ecclesiastical allegiance. Nothing in my life has been harder than to part company with my many friends. But I shall not try to describe at length my spiritual wrestlings, or the emotional struggles incident to this separation. Others have done it better than I can.

I have written the whole of this book as an Anglican. When I began it, over a year ago, I determined that I would make no change in my position until I had completed my case and had it before me in black and white. In the meantime I have been an interested observer of events in religious circles, whether Anglican or Roman Catholic. The current trend has but strengthened my conviction that Anglo-Catholicism is logically untenable, and that the hopes for the future of Christianity lie with the Churches that are in communion with Rome.

I still hold in affectionate esteem the Church which has guided and nourished me all these years. I owe an enormous debt to Anglicanism for teaching me to reverence the past, to keep my mind open to all that is best in modern scholarship, and to apply Christian principles to the social needs of humanity. My memory will always cherish the majestic rhythm, the calm cadences, and the rugged simplicity of the English of the Book of Common Prayer and the King James translation of the Bible. I have been especially favored in knowing many of the best representatives of the Anglican spirit—in this country and in England—true Christian Humanists, all of them. I can never forget what they have done for me. They rescued me from the arid deserts of sectarian Protestantism, and they have conducted me on my way until I could glimpse in the distance the Seven Hills of Rome.

S. P. D.

New York, June 7, 1930
Vigil of Pentecost.

WHY ROME

Chapter I

HESITATIONS AND DOUBTS

I

FOR thirty years I have been a priest in the Protestant Episcopal Church. In my childhood and youth I was a Presbyterian, as that was the family tradition. In my junior year at Harvard I took a history course in the first eight Christian centuries, under Professor Emerton, and I then discovered that the early Church bore little resemblance to the kind of Protestant Christianity in which I had been reared. I was asked to prepare a thesis on the subject of "The Epistles of St. Ignatius in Their Bearing on Early Church Organization," and it was my reading for that thesis that opened my eyes to the facts of early Church history. I realized that I must become a member of a Church that shared in the apostolic ministry. Under the influence of several High Church Episcopalians among my classmates, I became interested in the Church of the Advent in Boston, and after several months of instruction

under the Rector, Father Frisby, I was confirmed by
the Bishop of Massachusetts, Dr. Lawrence. From
that day on, I considered myself a High Churchman, or an Anglo-Catholic, and soon came to the
conclusion that I had a vocation to the priesthood.
Upon my graduation from Harvard in 1896, I became a postulant for holy orders under the Bishop
of Fond du Lac, Dr. Grafton, and after a three-
year course at the Western Theological Seminary in
Chicago, I was ordained deacon by the Bishop of
Chicago, Dr. McLaren, in May, 1899; and priest
by Bishop Grafton in December of the same year,
in the Cathedral of Fond du Lac, Wisconsin, which
was the town of my birth and early schooling.

I served first as Curate in St. John's Church, Rox-
bury, Boston; then as Vicar of St. Stephen's
Church, Menasha, Wis.; then as Rector of Grace
Church, Appleton, Wis., where I persuaded the
congregation to build a new church and change its
name to All Saints. In 1908 I became Dean of All
Saints' Cathedral, Milwaukee, where I remained
until 1915, when I came to New York to be Associ-
ate Rector under my old friend, Dr. Barry, at the
Church of St. Mary the Virgin. Recently, during
the years of his illness, I have been acting as Rector;
and was elected to that office January 1, 1929.
During eleven years of this period I was Editor

of the *American Church Monthly,* "a magazine of comment, criticism and review dealing with questions confronting the Anglican Communion, and more especially the Church in the United States."

During all this time I have supposed that I was a Catholic Christian. I have believed in the historical continuity of the Anglican Communion with the Catholic Church of the ages; I have regarded as essential, or highly desirable, such beliefs, institutions and practices as the historic episcopate, the priesthood, the seven sacraments, the Real Presence of Christ in the Eucharist, the Sacrifice of the Mass, fasting communion, prayers for the departed, the invocation of saints, devotions to our Lady, the use of the rosary, and so on. I have felt it devotionally helpful, though not essential, that the Liturgy should be in English rather than in Latin; that communion should be given in both kinds, that sacramental confession should be voluntary. I have acquiesced in a married clergy, though I preferred a celibate priesthood. In general, I have had the conviction that the Church should not compel her children to practice their religion in a prescribed way, but should leave them free to do as they liked. I have been temperamentally inclined to the belief that a hidebound system of orthodoxy ought not to be imposed rigorously on all the members of the Church, but that the truth of the Catholic faith should be demonstrated by Catholic scholars and that the Protestant-minded could be persuaded to accept it by appeals to their reason. I have always been an admirer of Bishop Gore, and he and other Anglo-Catholics of his school have had a profound effect in molding my religious convictions.

There was just one distinctive feature of the traditional system of Western Catholicism that I did not accept, and that was the Papacy. I have often said, when asked to define my position and the exigencies of the conversation demanded a brief reply, that I believed in Catholicism without the Pope. I was often conscious of a half-uttered reply emerging from the fringe of consciousness to the effect that this would be like playing Hamlet with Hamlet left out. Nevertheless, I comforted myself with the assurance that the Anglo-Catholic position was substantially that of the Orthodox Churches of the East, inasmuch as Orthodox theologians also rejected the modern Papal claims. As this seemed to me largely a matter of ecclesiastical organization rather than an essential principle of primitive Catholicism, I did not feel bound to regard it as an integral part of the Catholic system.

II

Nevertheless, from the very beginning of my ministry, I have suffered qualms of conscience on the subject of the Papacy. On the several occasions when I have thought I would like to marry, not the least of the considerations that have held me back from this heroic adventure was the thought that some day I might want to become a priest in the Roman Catholic Church. When friends of mine, both clerical and lay, have made their submission to Rome—and they have been many—I have often asked myself whether they were right and I was wrong. Whenever I have done any extended reading on the question I confess that I have not been able to dispel my doubts as completely as I might have wished. Such reading has proved so upsetting to my work, that I have often deferred it to a more convenient time. I have fallen back on the comforting assurance that I was not an historical scholar, and that wiser men than I appeared to be intellectually satisfied with the Anglican position. My immediate duty seemed to be to devote my energies to the multitudinous duties of my pastoral and editorial work. When temporarily troubled by the necessity of quieting others who were disturbed by Roman longings, I usually succeeded in concocting a plausible argument which appeared to satisfy them, even if it did not wholly satisfy me!

Obviously, this was not a comfortable position to settle down in, for it meant that I did not wholly believe in the anti-Roman case. Anyone who pretends to believe in the traditional Catholic religion, and yet rejects the Papacy, ought to be honestly convinced that the modern Papal claims are an unwarrantable addition to the Catholic faith. He ought to be able to show that they are unscriptural, unhistorical, uncatholic; and if they are all of these, and the Holy Spirit is guiding the Church, they should also be unworkable. In their treatment of the Papacy, Anglo-Catholic scholars have not always presented a united front. Some of them apparently accept the whole Papal position, infallibility and all the rest. Others are vague and inconclusive, and frequently dodge the issue. Yet the Papal claim to supreme jurisdiction is precisely the point that cannot be blithely ignored, for it constitutes the one important difference between Anglo-Catholicism and Roman Catholicism. If the Pope is right, then Anglo-Catholics are in an illogical position.

Indeed, almost all other Christians are quite convinced that Anglo-Catholics are ecclesiastical hybrids. Neither by Rome nor by Canterbury are they recognized as the authorized spokesmen for the Anglican Communion. They often speak as if all Anglicans were in complete sympathy with the Eastern Orthodox Churches, and as if both Anglicans and Orthodox stood like a solid phalanx for the pure Catholic faith against the arrogant pretensions of an autocratic Papacy. The truth is that the bulk of Anglicans throughout the world would be scandalized if anyone classed them as Catholics; and they regard the Eastern Orthodox as little better than superstitious heathen. It is somewhat disquieting to be classed by the majority of one's fellow-Churchmen, by non-episcopal Protestants and by Roman Catholics, as pseudo-Catholics and disloyal to the standards of the Protestant Episcopal Church. I must confess that I find it not altogether easy to justify my position when I read statements like the following from the pen of a Protestant Episcopal lawyer in the *Chronicle* of June, 1929:

Please state whether in the opinion of any honest man a concerted movement by members of a religious association to nullify the purposes of its organization, to teach doctrines which it condemns, and carry on practices which it forbids, should or should not be characterized by the same words (however ugly) as would be used in respect of a similar plot against the State, to wit, "conspiracy," "treason."

There can be no doubt that many extreme Anglo-Catholics are considered by the majority of Anglicans as traitors to the Anglican cause, and it would be difficult to prove that many priests that belong to this school are not playing fast and loose with their ordination vows.

Some years ago, during the controversy that arose over the public utterances of Dr. Percy Stickney Grant, I wrote an article to prove how necessary is the virtue of loyalty in the official representatives of the Church. As I did not publish this article, I may be pardoned for quoting from it the following paragraph: "It is generally agreed among the laity of the Church, if not so widely accepted among the clergy, that the authoritative teachers of the Church, who no longer believe in the creeds which they openly profess in the Church's worship, should resign their charges and ally themselves with some religious organization whose tenets they whole-heartedly accept. There is a great variety of religious organizations in America, ranging all the way from the Roman Catholic Church and the Eastern Orthodox Churches, to the Unitarians and the Community Church. Their range of credal requirements is so wide that a man must be a very eccentric thinker who cannot find in this religious Babel a creed that exactly fits his idiosyncracies. No doubt, it would mean a considerable sacrifice for a man to resign the rectorship of an important parish, with all the social prestige, perquisites and emoluments attached thereto, and throw in his lot with a radical sect, not conspicuous for its social standing. But surely none of our leading ecclesiastics are in the ministry for the social and financial rewards it may bring them. 'Better a dinner of herbs where love is, than a stalled ox and hatred therewith.' "

How about those of us who call ourselves Anglo-Catholics? Are not we also out of place? Are not we disloyal to the traditions of the Protestant Episcopal Church, and seeking to undermine by all sorts of subterfuges "the pure doctrines of the blessed Reformation"? Most of our ecclesiastical brethren think we are. Either by direct invitation or by sly innuendo they urge us almost daily to submit to the Pope. It is extremely distasteful to any sensitive person to remain for long in a place where he is not wanted, where most of his fellows regard him with suspicion, and a few with open contempt. It is like belonging to a social club where one is being ostracized by most of the members, and is conscious that they are secretly watching for an excuse to oust him.

Perhaps there is some truth in this charge of disloyalty. I tried it out the other day on one of my friends. I said to him, "You know perfectly well that you have not in your heart the least atom of loyalty to the Protestant Episcopal Church." He admitted it without argument, but insisted that he was loyal to Catholicism, and that his chief aim was to make the Catholic elements in the Anglican Communion triumphant over the Protestant elements. There are very few of the old-fashioned High Churchmen left, who gloried in belonging to the Episcopal Church. They studiously avoided using the term "Protestant," and hoped the day would soon come when it would be eliminated from the title-page of the Prayer Book. They designated that small fragment of Christendom to which they belonged as "the Church," and calmly ignored the Protestant denominations, the Roman Catholic Church and the Eastern Orthodox Churches as if they did not exist. My Presbyterian up-bringing kept me from rising to such heights of exclusiveness. I could never quite bring myself to use the term "Churchman" to designate a member of the Episcopal Church.

III

Ever since I began my ministry I have had to meet objections and criticisms from the members of my flock in regard to Catholic teaching and practices. I have been assailed from the right and from the left, for being too "High Church," too Catholic, or too pro-Roman. The practices for which I have been criticized have been such things as these: the liturgical use of incense; the adoption of colored Eucharistic vestments (no one seems to object to vestments, if only they are white); the hearing of confessions and the erection of a confessional in a new church; the substitution of the late Eucharist for Matins; the tone of voice used in celebrating Mass as either too loud or not loud enough; the daily Mass; processional lights; votive candles before a shrine; the use of the Hail Mary or the Rosary; public devotions to the Blessed Sacrament; devotions to the Sacred Heart of Jesus; the observance of days of fasting and abstinence; the Stations of the Cross; the Reservation of the Blessed Sacrament; the introduction of unfamiliar hymns; and so on, *ad infinitum*. I could fill a book with the catalogue of these practices.

People do not object so much to the teaching and preaching of Catholic doctrine; it is only when they are expected to do something which shows they believe in it that they rise in revolt. There is nothing that Episcopalians dislike so much as being jolted out of their ordinary routine. They love the

"dear old services" to which they have long been
accustomed. One old lady refused to come to church
any more after the church had been renovated, because, as she said, "A hardwood floor is too High
Church for me!" One of my wardens—an Englishman, by the way—in complaining to me about
a confessional having been put up in the new
church I had induced them to build, said to me,
"The whole town is *ringing* with it, and my friends
twit me by asking when I am going to confession."
When I left to go to another parish, the confessional
was removed.

It cannot be denied that this is an extraordinary
experience for one who professes to be a Catholic
priest, and whose lot has always been cast in what
are known as Catholic dioceses or parishes. Is it any
wonder that I am tempted to question the Catholicity of the Episcopal Church?

For thirty years now I have had abundant opportunity to make an intimate study of the Episcopal
Church. I have had a wide acquaintance with its
clergy and laity, both in their external activities
and in their inner spiritual experiences. I have also
made careful observations of the development of
the Catholic Movement in the whole Anglican
Communion. In consequence, I begin to entertain
serious doubts whether the Anglican Church is

really an organic part of the Catholic Church, except in so far as any group of baptized Christians may be said to belong to the soul of the Catholic Church. It is much easier to believe that it is one of the separated Churches which are the offspring of the Reformation, cut off from the center and source of unity.

IV

For some years I have been deeply disturbed over conditions among the clergy in the American Episcopal Church who call themselves Anglo-Catholics. Not that conditions are by any means ideal among the rest of the clergy of this Church; but it is the Anglo-Catholics in particular that I have known from the inside. I could mention scores of priests who have collapsed during the past few years. Some have lost their faith, and given up the ministry; some have retired from active parochial duties, and are doing other kinds of work or traveling for their health; some have undergone serious moral disintegration; some have broken down nervously or been incapacitated by other forms of illness. I am acquainted with not a few who are struggling against enormous odds, are experiencing continual searchings of heart, are sad and gloomy, and are apparently on the verge of some kind of explosion.

I keep asking myself, what is wrong? Surely it cannot be that all the Anglo-Catholic clergy are weak-minded and incompetent. Many of them are men of attractive personality, and highly gifted intellectually and spiritually. Nor can all these sad cases be accounted for by the admitted strain of keeping up one's faith in a sceptical and machine-worshipping age. The mental conflict of faith with unbelief is today especially acute. But that cannot wholly explain the situation. I am driven to the conclusion that the real explanation is to be found in the ecclesiastical system under which we are working.

We are trying to live and act as Catholic priests when our ecclesiastical superiors, most of our brethren in the ministry, the bulk of the laity and the general public regard us as Protestant clergymen. Some are endeavoring also to live the celibate life, in spite of the fact that many of the women they meet look upon them as fair game in the matrimonial chase. We are engaged in the difficult occupation of trying to accommodate ourselves to uncongenial surroundings, like fitting square pegs into round holes. We are walking in one direction, while our faces are turned in the opposite direction, and we think we are going that way. We are paddling our canoes against a swift current, and our strength is soon exhausted. We are spending our energies in converting Protestants into somewhat feeble and halting Catholics while the prevailing official tendency in the Episcopal Church is to keep her people Protestant and lead them to fraternize with the Protestant denominations.

In this heart-breaking task we have no authority to uphold us. Indeed, we often find ourselves in conflict with the lawful authorities under whom we have pledged ourselves to serve. We talk vaguely of the authority of the Catholic Church, when the one consistent voice of Catholic authority in the twentieth century proceeds from Rome. When we tell our people that the Catholic Church teaches thus and so on any point of doctrine or morals, we mean the Roman Catholic Church. Anglo-Catholic priests who hear confessions are compelled to resort to Roman Catholic handbooks on moral theology and casuistry because there are few Anglican books that cover the ground.

What it all comes to is that every Anglo-Catholic priest is a law unto himself. He interprets the Bible and the Prayer Book in his own way, and follows his own individualistic whims in arranging the services and ceremonial in his parish church. There is no consensus of opinion on ritual and ornaments among Anglicans, except in the small pro-Roman group, who meticulously adhere to the Baltimore Ceremonial of the Roman Catholic Church. I have never pretended to be a liturgical expert. I merely observe what has been arranged by others before me, except for a few changes now and then to accommodate our worship to the current styles in vogue among Anglo-Catholics. Thus every priest must carry on his shoulders a tremendous burden of responsibility, and it is not surprising that many break down under the load.

Can it be self-interest and pride that have blinded us to the conclusion that this is an absurd situation? We have been caught in the toils of a movement which once had high promise, but now appears to have lost its way. We do not like to admit that we were mistaken, when in the enthusiastic days of our youth we threw in our lot with Anglo-Catholicism. Many of us hold prominent positions which we hesitate to relinquish. In middle age or later it is not easy to find new jobs that will support us. Many of the clergy are married and have children, and they must carry on for the sake of their families. It takes real moral courage under the circumstances to admit that to be Catholics we must be in communion with the See of Peter, and that we have undertaken a hopeless task in trying to transform the Protestant Episcopal Church into an American province of the Catholic Church. It is not so easy even to keep a foothold for ourselves. Why keep on with this Quixotic enterprise when most Episcopalians want to be Protestants, and there is a perfectly satisfactory and flourishing Catholic church around the corner? Is it sound wisdom to continue the fight against such overwhelming odds until we drop in our tracks with nothing permanent accomplished?

Chapter II

THINGS WHICH CANNOT BE SHAKEN

I

I AM writing this chapter on board the SS. Berengaria. This is the third time I have crossed on this ship. My religious experiences on board have laid bare certain deficiencies in the practical system of the Anglican Church. So far as I could discover, no arrangements were ever made by the ship's authorities for a celebration of the Holy Communion on Sunday. When I crossed last summer I requested the chief steward to announce on the bulletin board Saturday that there would be a Communion Service Sunday morning at eight, and he kindly agreed to give the proper facilities. He did not post the notice, however, until about nine o'clock Saturday evening. Whether for that reason, or because there were no communicants of the Anglican Church among the eight hundred first cabin passengers who cared to make their communion on the Lord's Day, there was no congregation when I went to the improvised altar at eight o'clock on Sunday morning. Consequently I did not celebrate. There was a large congregation present at eleven o'clock Matins, conducted by the ship's officers, with the Union Jack and the Stars and Stripes as the only visible symbols to suggest the nature of the proceedings. A visitor from Japan might have concluded that this was primarily a patriotic rite which mentioned God only incidentally.

There was a Roman Catholic Mass at nine o'clock, in the second cabin, which I attended. It was unmistakably a Christian act of worship in which crowds of worshippers took part with reverence and devotion. I was impressed by the fact that on this great ship, one of the leading British transatlantic liners, England's Established Church had made no provision for the Lord's service of the Eucharist on the Lord's Day—the only act of worship which Christ ordained and commanded us to offer. There were doubtless hundreds of communicants of the Church of England and the American Episcopal Church on board. But none of them had sufficient interest in sacramental religion to request that an opportunity be given them to make their communions. I am not accusing the Cunard Line of being responsible for this condition of things. It affords, however, a striking commentary on the kind of religion that is propagated by the Anglican Church.

Is it unfair to draw the conclusion that the Church of England is only a department of the State, and exists chiefly to promote loyalty to the Empire and moral respectability among her subjects? The religious activities of the Anglican Church appear to be extremely weak and superficial. The clergy are mostly English gentlemen of the upper classes whose chief devotion is to their class and country. They and, to a greater extent, the laity give the impression of being Englishmen first, and Christians afterwards. They acquiesce in the appointment of their bishops by the Prime Minister, even though he happen to be a Baptist or a Presbyterian. They permit the House of Commons to decide whether they shall revise their book of worship, or not.

Several years ago, when the Prince of Wales was visiting in New York, the chaplain of the battleship on which he was traveling paid a visit to my church. I asked the chaplain if he would like to have a visitor's card at my club, and he said he would appreciate it very much. I met him at luncheon one day in the club, and he complained of the many things he had to do that afternoon. I asked if I could be of any assistance to him. "Well," he replied, "one of the things that is troubling me

most is that I must procure some gin for his Royal
Highness. He is giving a dinner party this evening
on the ship, and has no gin for the cocktails." I
confess I was somewhat surprised to learn that it
was one of the duties of the chaplain to supply gin
for the royal dinners, but said I would see what I
could do for him. Whether or not I succeeded in
getting the gin is no part of this story, which is
meant as a parable of the relations of Church and
State in England.

All of which leads me to ask why I should be so
closely associated with England in the practice of
my religion. I am not an Englishman, but an American. For seven generations my paternal ancestors
and for fourteen generations my maternal ancestors
have been Americans. The Protestant Episcopal
Church was, before the Revolution, the Church of
England in the American Colonies, and shamefully
neglected by the Mother Church. For a century and
a half before the Revolution no bishop was sent to
our shores. The sacrament of confirmation was
not administered during that length of time, and
candidates for holy orders were compelled to
make the long and dangerous journey to England to
be ordained. What wonder that the Methodists
and Congregationalists and Presbyterians made
rapid progress in the Colonies! After the Revolu-

tion the Church of England took no steps to provide bishops for the new national Church—now staggering under the cumbersome title "Protestant Episcopal." In all likelihood the Mother Church never would have sent us bishops had not Dr. Seabury, of Connecticut, taken things into his own hands and persuaded the Scottish episcopate to consecrate him our first bishop. Such niggardly treatment from our ecclesiastical forbears in England merits little gratitude.

Even now the Catholic-minded members of the Protestant Episcopal Church, like the heirs of the Oxford Movement in England, must—if they are to be understood—call themselves Anglo-Catholics. But why "Anglo"? If they are English then they are not Catholic; if Catholic they are international or supernational, but not English. There is some ground for using the term "Roman Catholic," because the Petrine claims of the Bishop of Rome have always been an essential part of that system. This does not mean that she is exclusively identified with the City or Empire of Rome. Her supernational character has now been proclaimed to all the world through the Vatican Settlement, whereby the Bishop of Rome becomes indeed a supernational figure, independent of any earthly government. That is as it should be. The Catholic Church should

be above all national distinctions, and unhampered
by national loyalties. Her primary loyalty is to
Jesus Christ the King.

II

To come back to the ship, there is just one form
of religion that seems to be able to carry on, week
in and week out, aboard all the transatlantic liners,
and that is the Roman Catholic religion. All other
sects and Churches lapse into silence and fade away
into insignificance when one embarks upon the sea.
On almost every ocean steamship there is a Roman
Catholic Mass on Sunday morning, and often on
every day of the week. On the English ships the
clergy who are officially recognized as priests by
the Church of England are not only not asked to
celebrate Holy Communion, but they are ignored
at the official religious service on Sunday. The cap-
tain, purser and chief steward are the only officiants
allowed to take part in this almost pontifical glor-
ification of British patriotism. Possibly it is not regarded as an act of Christian worship, but only as
the chief rite of the religion of nationalism.

Just as in a small way the ocean liners have put
modern religions to the test and demonstrated the
abiding worth of Catholicism, so in a much larger

way did the World War. Whenever people are
turned loose from the restraining influences of a
fixed social order, all forms of Christianity seem to
dissolve into nothingness except Roman Catholicism. When heaven and earth are shaken only the
things that cannot be shaken remain. The Church
that is founded upon the rock of Peter stands se-
cure. The gates of hell cannot prevail against it.

When the American forces went forth to take
their places beside the Allies on the French front,
the chaplains who were commissioned to look after
their spiritual welfare were divided into three
groups: Catholic, Protestant and Jewish. The Protestant Episcopal Church was naturally classed as
one of the Protestant denominations. However
Catholic her chaplains might have been in their
convictions and in their parochial practices at
home, while in the army they had to minister to all
kinds of Protestants on a common basis. They found
that it was expected of them that they should give
Holy Communion to all Protestants who desired it,
whether they had been baptized or not. They had
to conduct religious services which would be acceptable to all, evangelistic services of prayer and
praise. The Anglican communion service as the
chief act of worship would have been unintelligible
to most of the men in their regiments. In conse-

quence their work was mainly of a secular character, and differed little from the work of Y. M. C. A. secretaries. They were authorized by the Government to act as Protestant chaplains, and all ecclesiastical theories had to make way for cold facts. It was a condition, not a theory, that confronted them. They were plunged into compulsory Pan-Protestantism with a vengeance.

Here again the Roman Catholic Church was unhampered. Her chaplains were enabled to carry on their religious work exactly on the lines commanded by their Church, and in loyalty to her principles. They celebrated Mass daily, heard confessions, communicated their men with the Reserved Sacrament before they went over the top, and gave them their Viaticum in the hour of their death. The War was the supreme test. The religious foundations of Protestantism crumbled in the day of battle. Only the foundations laid by God endured the strain.

III

In a larger sense the World War has proved a fiery trial for the forces of Christendom. The refining fire has made manifest the nature of the religious structures which men have built upon the one Foundation, Jesus Christ. Some have been built of wood, hay or stubble, and are now being destroyed before our eyes. Others have been built of gold, silver or precious stones, and they remain.

In the eleven years that have elapsed since Armistice Day, profound changes have taken place in the Protestant world. In Germany the Lutheran Church has been disestablished, and with the loss of State support the Protestant forces throughout the Reich have rapidly disintegrated. The clergy have been reduced to poverty, schools and other religious institutions have been forced to close their doors, and hundreds of thousands of German Protestants have been converted to Catholicism. The Catholic Center Party has become the controlling party of the German nation. Catholic schools have been immensely strengthened, and the land in which the Protestant Reformation had its origin has become one of the most vigorous Catholic strongholds in the modern world. Professor Gavin of the General Theological Seminary, in an article on "Contemporary Religion in Germany," in *Theology* for November, 1929, says:

The chief battle of German religion today, Protestant as well as Catholic, has to do with the very foundations of Christian theism and elementary Christian ethics. The tragedy of the situation is that religious forces cannot combine to meet the subversive and direct attacks of the new religion from Leningrad. It is difficult to avoid the conclusion that in many parts of the German-speaking world the one organized force which can cope effectively with the disruptive and challenging propaganda from Russia is Roman Catholicism. The bases of Protestant unity which were maintained before the War have long since been destroyed, and German Protestantism has not by its history been prepared to meet this new emergency with unified power.

In Switzerland, Holland and Denmark the ranks of Protestantism are being rapidly depleted through unbelief and birth-control, whereas the Catholic Church is steadily increasing in numbers. In England the Established Church has been prevented by Parliament from issuing her own revised Prayer Book, and is consequently in a very precarious position. If the bishops persist in the face of Parliamentary opposition and put the new Prayer Book into common use, their action is quite likely to lead to disestablishment. The controversy over the revised Prayer Book and the fact that the Church is being dictated to by the State have unsettled the faith of many devout adherents of the Church, and there have in consequence been many conversions to Rome. Anglo-Catholics have been divided by this controversy, the more advanced section insisting on devotions to the Reserved Sacrament, which the new Prayer Book forbids, while the more moderate section has discontinued these devotions at the behest of the timorous bishops. In any case, the Anglo-Catholic cause appears to have received a severe set-back.

In contrast to these conditions in the strongholds of Protestantism, the position of the Papacy has been immensely solidified and strengthened since the War. Whereas before the War only a few nations sent diplomatic representatives to the Vatican, there are now ambassadors at the Vatican from practically every nation in Europe and the Americas, except the United States. This means that the Pope is now the spokesman for Christianity to most of the nations of the world. Since the Vatican settlement the Pope is an independent sovereign and not subject to the dictates of any secular government. The World War removed the three greatest obstacles to the spread of Papal influence: the Kaiser, the Czar and the Khalif. The next great step in the progress of Roman Catholicism will be reunion with the Orthodox Churches of the East. With the Czar out of the way that end may quite conceivably be attained in the next generation. The Church in Russia, in particular, would be greatly strengthened in her dealings with the anti-religious Soviet government if backed by the international forces of Roman Catholicism. In France the position of the Papacy has become more favorable owing to its disciplinary measures against the reactionary Royalists and its greater sympathy with the democratic elements in the Republic. In Mexico the three-year conflict between Church and State has been terminated through the harmonizing counsels of Ambassador Morrow.

It is argued by some that the last election proved that a Roman Catholic cannot be elected President of the United States. It undoubtedly did prove that Roman Catholics do not yet constitute a majority of American voters, if we assume that all Roman Catholics voted for Governor Smith. It is extremely difficult to prove that the religious issue was the determining issue in the election. It would seem more likely that what the election really demonstrated was that a Tammany Democrat who was opposed to Prohibition could not be elected President. It is quite possible that if Mr. Hoover had been a Roman Catholic and Governor Smith a Protestant, the result would have been the same. This, however, is only my own personal opinion, and I know that there are many who take a different view.

The day may not be far off when Roman Catholics will be in the majority among American Christians. If this comes about it will be because of their marriage laws, their large families, their schools and colleges which are training the young to become intelligent Catholics, and the steady stream of conversions from the ranks of Protestantism. Nevertheless, as the majority of Americans are pagans, it will probably be a long time before the United States is a Roman Catholic country.

The growth of the Roman Catholic Church in the United States during the past thirty years has been extraordinary. This is borne out by the facts of the religious census. Moreover, no one with ordinary powers of perception can help noticing how in the cities and all through the country districts her far-seeing ecclesiastical leaders are obtaining the most advantageous sites for their churches and their educational and charitable institutions. Whether or not they have the harmlessness of doves, they at least have the wisdom of serpents. They are gaining wide publicity through the public press, and they make clever use of the radio. The War helped them in many ways, as I have indicated, and since the War they have been making tremendous strides. Whatever one may think of the Irish and their predominating influence in American Catholicism, no one can deny that under Irish leadership the Roman Church has prospered enormously in America.

The growing strength of Roman Catholicism

since the War does not of course necessarily prove that Rome is right, or that her influence will continue to spread. The prestige of the Roman Papacy in Western Europe during the Middle Ages did not prevent the secession of the Northern countries at the time of the Protestant Reformation. Every institution has its ups and downs in the course of its history, and it may be that Catholicism under the Pope will enter another period of eclipse in the latter half of this century. God alone knows. Nevertheless, no man can help being impressed by the historical trends of his own age. *Non haec sine numine Divum eveniunt.* For thirty years I have been trying to interpret the signs of the times. Events have not turned out favorably to the cause to which I committed myself when I was ordained. Rather, they have persistently pointed in the direction of Rome. Is it only an hallucination, or do I hear a voice saying to me, "It is hard for thee to kick against the pricks"?

Chapter III

SECESSIONS OR CONVERSIONS?

I

ONE of the most heart-breaking experiences of an Anglo-Catholic pastor is the blow he receives on learning that members of his flock are submitting to Rome. Every time it happens—and it has happened often in my pastoral career—it suggests pointedly to his mind the question whether he too should change his ecclesiastical allegiance. As a rule these converts to Rome are among the most faithful members of the parish, and have been practicing their religion conscientiously for many years; and now they conclude that they have been in the wrong place all along! They become dissatisfied with the Anglican Church for all sorts of reasons. They are troubled by the fact that persecution at the hands of the authorities is levelled chiefly at the Catholic-minded clergy; they find themselves in a parish where they are deprived of the privilege of making their communions early on Sunday or of going to confession; they are upset by the utterances of a prominent bishop or priest which are subversive of the faith; or they read in the newspapers that one of the leading Eastern dioceses has elected successively five Liberal or ultra-Protestant clergymen to the office of bishop-coadjutor, and that each has declined the election. It is such occurrences as these that fill their minds with doubt as to the Catholicity of the Anglican Church.

Such doubts are not easily dispelled. These people may be told that the Anglican Church has never yet officially fallen into heresy; that the existence of the Catholic Movement is a proof that this communion is still a living branch of the Catholic Church; that the Catholic faith and Catholic devotions are increasingly tolerated by the authorities; and that it is their duty to remain where God has placed them and work for the spread of Catholic faith and practice in their own communion. Such arguments may convince them, or they may not. They may reply that they do not feel that it is their vocation to convert the bishops and other clergy to the faith which they are professedly commissioned to uphold. In any case, while such arguments may appeal to those who have been reared as Episcopalians, they cannot so easily be pressed upon intelligent adults who are being prepared for confirmation. Why should they enlist in a campaign to Catholicize the members of the Protestant Episcopal Church? Why not present themselves at once for confirmation in the Roman Catholic Church, where Catholics do not need to be on the defensive? Such questions are difficult to answer.

In losing to Rome devout souls of high spiritual capacity, we are being deprived of those who constitute the spiritually sound and healthy nucleus of our flock. The cream is being skimmed off, and the milk that is left is often very thin. Neither sheep-raisers nor dairymen could view long-continued processes of that sort with complacency. A few such losses take the heart out of a Catholic-minded priest, and make him feel that he is playing a losing game. It is not as if these people were deserting to the world, the flesh and the devil. In that case he would have no compunction against going after them and trying to lead them back into the fold. But when his sheep have once browsed in the green and peaceful pastures of a world-wide Catholicism it seems cruel to drag them back to the shell-strewn battleground of Anglicanism.

It may be said in reply that those who transfer their allegiance to Rome are only an insignificant fraction of the membership of the Anglican Church. That may be true, but it is this small persistent fraction that continues to sap the strength of the Anglo-Catholic movement. When anything happens in the Anglican Communion that is distasteful to the Catholic-minded, like the controversy that arose over Dr. Percy Stickney Grant, the opening of the pulpits of our cathedrals and other churches to non-episcopal ministers, the published attacks of the Bishop of Birmingham on sacramental religion, the proposed South Indian scheme for Church unity, the proscription by the English bishops of public devotions to the Sacrament reserved, or the publication of lives of our Lord by prominent New York rectors which treat the Gospel accounts of His Virgin Birth and Resurrection as fabulous tales without any historical value; this small fraction is immeasurably increased. Little drops of water will wear away a stone, and this continuous succession of conversions to Rome is paralyzing the Anglo-Catholic movement.

II

Some of my former parishioners who have become Roman Catholics have been of the type commonly referred to as neurotic. I have labored with them long and arduously, in the confessional and out of it, to try to help them dissolve their com-

plexes or conquer their phobias—but in vain. It
has been one of the most perplexing problems in my
ministry that the faithful practice of their religion
did not seem to help these unfortunate souls. I have
in several cases made careful inquiries from their
friends as to how they have since fared in the Roman Church; and the answer has been that they
appear to be radiantly happy and at peace. The
transformation that has taken place in their lives
bears some psychological resemblance to those conversions from sin which one reads of in books like
Harold Begbie's *Twice-Born Men*. How are we to
account for it? It cannot of course be interpreted
as demonstrating that they did not receive grace
from the sacraments of the Episcopal Church, and
that Anglican orders are therefore invalid. It may
be that the reasons why nervous people do not fare
well as Anglo-Catholics are their consciousness of
the instability of their position within the Anglican
Communion, the necessity of continually being on
the defensive, and the self-consciousness involved
in their distinctive religious practices. These things
are hard for even normal people to bear. The fact
remains that in Rome they have no longer any feeling of instability; they are not compelled to be on
the defensive; and they are not self-conscious whenever they genuflect, recite the Rosary, or make the

sign of the cross. This is in itself an argument for Rome, whatever one may think about the comparative efficacy of Roman and Anglican sacraments.

I am reminded of the personal testimony made to me by a highly educated man who long occupied an honored position in the ministry of the American Episcopal Church, and has now been a Roman Catholic for nearly ten years. He told me that since his submission to Rome he has never felt the slightest doubt about any matter of faith, or about the reality of the sacramental grace that he is receiving; and that his whole Anglican past seems to have dropped out of his consciousness like a forgotten dream. To me the significant point in this testimony is that all the years of sacramental experience in the Episcopal Church were to him as if they had never been.

While hearing confessions a terrible suspicion has often projected itself from the dark regions of the unconscious into my conscious thinking, that many penitents who have been under my care for years give the impression, as they tell of their spiritual struggles and failures, that they are receiving no help at all from God. It is as if everything depended on their own efforts. They appear to be waging an uphill fight, and they often grow weary and discouraged. Why do they not gain more strength from their absolutions and communions? I do not know. Why is it that in so many of those who have tried to live faithfully the Catholic life the fruits of sacramental religion seem to be so meager? Far from developing such distinctive virtues of Catholic sanctity as humility, meekness, obedience, charity, they might simply have been good pagans. I have often been puzzled by the fact that pride, harshness, uncharitableness, and an uncontrolled temper are so common among men and women who have grown old in the Episcopal Church and partaken frequently of its sacraments. As for the more devout of our young men and women, their pious practices do not seem to produce the moral and spiritual attractiveness that might reasonably be expected. They are often pharisaical and contemptuous toward those who do not practice the minutiæ of external worship exactly as they do. Even Anglo-Catholics among the clergy are not always conspicuous for humility and patience.

I do not wish to enter upon the task of making invidious comparisons between the type of character to be found among Roman Catholics, on the one hand, and Anglo-Catholics or Protestants, on the other. Saints and sinners can be found among all groups of Christians, whether Catholic or Protestant. Unfortunately, no religion is a guarantee of lovable character in all its adherents. If all Roman Catholics were humble, kindly, generous, patient, pure-minded, sober and unselfish; and all Anglicans and Protestants were proud, over-bearing, pharisaical, harsh, covetous, gluttonous and sensual; there would be no further room for argument about ecclesiastical differences. Everybody would submit to the Pope.

I have, however, often been distressed by the fact that the Anglican Church does not commemorate in her calendar any saints that have developed within her communion since the Reformation. I suppose the reason is not that there have been no Anglican saints, but that the bishops, the National Assembly of the Church of England, or the General Convention of the American Episcopal Church could not agree as to who were to be canonized. We can imagine the angry protests that would burst forth if an attempt were made to beatify even Philip Bouverie Pusey, John Keble, A. H. Mackonochie, Robert Dolling, Charles Chapman Grafton or Sturges Allen. The Anglican authorities could never agree on the canonization of a single saint, so perhaps it is just as well that it has not been seriously attempted. Somehow, one gets the impression that Liberal and Evangelical Churchmen are not devoted

to the saints. They tolerate them, but are suspicious
of them. Perhaps they are afraid that veneration of
the saints may lead to putting them in the place of
God as objects of worship. If they ever outgrow
this hagiophobia they may some day venerate the
Gloomy Dean as a saint. Perhaps, also, Henry Major
might fulfill their expectations in this direction.
American Broad Churchmen of the future may
erect shrines in honor of St. Alexander of Pough-
keepsie, St. William of the Bowery or St. Robert of
Park Avenue.

III

I have said that one of the chief reasons why
Anglo-Catholics secede from their own communion and become Roman Catholics is that while traveling or when they are compelled to live perma-
nently in a town where the Episcopal Church gives
them anything but a hearty welcome and deprives
them of the Catholic privileges to which they have
been accustomed, they always find a Roman Catholic church near at hand where they can at least
fulfill their duty of attending Mass. This practice
may very easily lead them to making a complete
submission to the authority of Rome. I have heard
of Anglicans who, under such circumstances, feel

justified in making their confessions to a Roman
Catholic priest and receiving the Blessed Sacrament
at his hands, without letting him know their real
ecclesiastical status. That does not seem like dealing
fairly with the Roman Church, and such action
must vitiate the effects of the sacraments which
they receive. In dealing with people who are troubled by the failure of the Anglican Church to minister to their spiritual needs, I have tried to convince
them that while they might attend a Roman Mass
when their own Church provided no Mass except
on the first Sunday of the month, their duty was to
use to the full such spiritual privileges as were provided in their own Church and pray daily for the
spread of the Catholic Movement in the Anglican
Communion. In this connection I have often used
the argument that there are three historic schools
of thought which have a proper place within the
confines of Anglicanism: the Catholic, the Liberal
and the Evangelical. Each school stands for valuable principles: the Catholic for historical continuity and sacramentalism; the Liberal for an attempt
to translate the Christian faith into modern language and to make it acceptable to the modern
mind; the Evangelical for loyalty to the Gospel.
The Church of England has always stood for this
wide comprehensiveness. I am now convinced that

this argument is fallacious. It is not right that the Church should be divided into segments, each emphasizing one or more phases of the Catholic religion. That means always that the laity in each place are being cheated out of something to which they have a right. The true way to phrase the argument for comprehensiveness would be somewhat as follows: the Church as a whole and every individual in the Church, whether priest or layman, should stand for all three elements of religion which have been so admirably expounded by Baron von Huegel in the first chapter of his great work, *The Mystical Element in Religion*: the Institutional, the Intellectual, and the Mystical. That is one way of describing Catholicism. The Catholic Church has always been apostolic, sacramental, reasonable, adaptable, evangelical and mystical. If the Episcopal Church in any particular place is lacking in any of these elements, she is by that very fact something less than Catholic.

IV

Occasionally some of my friends have used the argument that if the Anglican Church is a training school for Rome I ought to be satisfied, for in that case I am shepherding the lost sheep and leading

them back into the one fold presided over by St.
Peter. This seems to me a very feeble reason for remaining in the ministry of the Anglican Church. I
cannot regard myself as a shepherd whose only
function is to lead the lost sheep back into the fold.
By the terms of my ordination I am a shepherd of
all the sheep, a pastor of the whole flock committed
to my care, not simply of those that are lost. It is
my privilege, as well as my duty, to lead all my sheep
into the green pastures, and feed them beside the
waters of comfort.

*Parasti in conspectu meo mensam, adversus
eos qui tribulant me.*
*Impinguasti in oleo caput meum: et calix meus
inebrians quam praeclarus est!*
*Et misericordia tua subsequetur me omnibus
diebus vitae meae:*
*Et ut inhabitem in domo Domini, in longitu-
dinem dierum.*

Either the Catholic Apostolic and Roman Church
is the one fold or she is not. If she is, I am not content to remain on the outside for the remainder of
my days, however many wandering sheep I may
direct into her peaceful fold. If she is not, because
the Anglican Church is an integral part of the

Catholic Church, temporarily separated through no fault of her own from the center of unity, then it is the duty of Anglicans to remain where they are and work for reunion with Rome. That is the dilemma which every Anglo-Catholic must honestly face; he cannot dangle interminably on both its horns.

One of my friends has written me as follows: "I don't believe you would find the Roman Church a solution. Agnosticism would be far better. In Rome you would be retreating into a more obscurantist position, and getting more involved instead of more simplified. You have the childlike feeling that somewhere there must be *the* perfect way of life—the true solution—the magic formula—when as a matter of fact everything is hopelessly entangled and we shall probably not see the real way out till the next world."

Yes, I confess I have that childlike feeling that somewhere there must be *the* perfect way of life. In the Anglican Church I seem to have found everything hopelessly entangled. Because of my faith in God, and in the wisdom of our Divine Lord in founding his Church on earth, and His promise that the Holy Spirit would guide her into all the truth, I believe that *the* perfect way of life exists in this world, and that the wayfaring man, though a fool, may find it and not err therein. Our Lord certainly promised that He would found a Church that would be indefectible. "On this rock I will build my Church, and the gates of hell shall not prevail against it." I refuse to be bamboozled by the arbitrary assumption of Modernist critics that this saying is an interpolation of a later time.

Chapter IV

AFTER THIRTY YEARS

I

INASMUCH as I have realized most of the factors in the situation for thirty years, and have been intermittently troubled by doubts from the beginning of my ministry, why should I at this late date decide that my conscience will not permit me to be content with Anglicanism any longer? Thus have queried some of my friends.

In every life there are all sorts of emotional considerations which make it difficult to formulate an intellectual decision. When one presumably has many years of life in this world before one, it is easy to postpone decisions to a more convenient occasion. As one grows older the need of coming to a decision becomes more pressing. Then too there have always been many people who relied upon me and looked to me for guidance. I did not want to unsettle them. It might throw them back into bleak Protestantism or sheer unbelief. I have now come to feel that in spite of such possibilities a spiritual leader or pastor owes it to his followers that he preserve his moral integrity and obey his conscience. They cannot blame him for doing what he believes to be right, especially when there are so many emotional obstacles standing in the way. It can do no permanent harm to any Christians, if they are driven seriously to reconsider their religious beliefs and ecclesiastical position, and make sure that they are neither blinding themselves nor following blind leaders.

Another reason why I have been reluctant to make a change is that I have felt that I had assumed responsibilities to the Catholic Movement in the Episcopal Church which I could not without great deliberation cast aside. Although I have no illusions as to my own importance, I know that if any man who is rector of a large city parish of the Episcopal Church should submit to Rome, it might quite conceivably hurt the cause with which he has been associated. For many years I have proceeded on the assumption that God had placed me in the Anglican ministry and was counting on me to help develop the Catholic Movement, so that some day the whole membership of the Anglican Church might be Catholic in convictions and practices, and then reunion with the rest of Catholic Christendom could soon become a reality.

Many things have happened during recent years to make me doubt the wisdom and truth of that assumption. I suppose the simplest explanation is that I have become disillusioned and discouraged with Anglo-Catholicism. It is not making headway. It is seriously divided into the two camps of the Pro-Romans and the Liberal Catholics. In England the movement has slumped badly since the failure to put through the revision of the Book of Common Prayer. The proposed new Prayer Book brought to light the cleavage that had long existed among Anglo-Catholics. Many of them welcomed the new book as a distinct improvement in a Catholic direction; while many others regarded it as a calamity because of its changes in the Communion Office and its restrictions on the devotional use of the Reserved Sacrament. In the American Episcopal Church the authorities are suspicious of the Catholic Movement; and many of the younger clergy, who have been trained in the seminaries to carry on their ministry along Catholic lines, find it difficult to obtain positions. Except for a few large parishes in the cities, the clergy of Catholic convictions are everywhere hampered and restricted by their vestries or bishops, though perhaps to a lesser degree than their brethren in England. In my own parochial and editorial work I have felt increasingly that I was walking back and forth in a blind alley, out of touch with the main flow of life in the Episcopal Church. Our religious orders are distrusted by the majority of the clergy and laity, and in consequence are gaining few recruits. There are many calls for them to take charge of broken down parishes, or to engage in slum work or missionary enterprises that the married clergy dare not touch; but they are unable to respond to most of these calls because their numbers are so small. In the earlier part of my life as a priest I was led on by all sorts of vain delusions and mirages. I thought there were many parishes and dioceses in the American Episcopal Church where the Catholic Movement was carrying all before it. I knew them only from the outside. Now I know the whole situation from within, and my eyes are open to the facts.

II

Moreover I have come to feel differently about its being my vocation to reform the Anglican Church, or even that small section of it known as the Protestant Episcopal Church in the United States of America. I have never forgotten those words of Dr. Kinsman in his *Salve Mater:* "It is certainly a great relief to exchange the task of trying to reform the Church—the necessary effort for all who hold my former point of view—for the simpler one of letting the Church try to reform me!" (p. 294.) That strikes the note of real Christian humility. It cannot but engender in the Anglo-Catholic clergy an unwholesome pride for them to think that they alone are walking in the right path, and that the mass of the clergy and laity of their Church are groping blindly in the dark forest of Protestantism. It is because of this pretension that we are so often despised and hated by our fellow Churchmen. They refuse to act as the clay models on which we are to perform our ecclesiastical experiments.

If Anglo-Catholics used only the services prescribed in the Prayer Book, and regarded them as sufficiently suitable forms for Catholic worship, they might be tolerated. That was the view of the Prayer Book which I held for many years, as is evident in the chapters which I wrote in *The Religion of the Prayer Book,* in collaboration with Dr. Barry. Subsequently, under the insistent pressure of our pro-Roman brethren, and impelled by the fear of being called old-fashioned, amiably desirous also of pleasing our constituents, many of us have shifted our position. The more advanced of the younger clergy of the Catholic Movement now act on the quite probable assumption that the Prayer Book is inadequately Catholic and marred by Protestant blemishes. Therefore they splint it and bandage it with interpolations from the Roman Mass, Benediction of the Blessed Sacrament, the Litany of the Saints, the Rosary, the Mass of the Pre-Sanctified, the Veneration of the Cross, and so on to an ever increasing degree. The old Book of Common Prayer is now quite useless as a missal on our altars.

Who are we, that we should presume to alter and supplement the Prayer Book forms of worship, in the teeth of the ecclesiastical authorities to which at our ordination we promised obedience? Many of my clerical brethren would have no hesitation in answering, "We are the self-appointed reformers of the Anglican Church, commissioned by God to lead her back into the fullness of Catholic faith and worship." Could pride and conceit be more full-blown than that?

What is all this but the philosophy of childishness and immaturity? The successful passage from infancy into maturity depends, so the psychiatrists tell us, on the breaking up and reconstruction of those habits which were appropriate only to our earliest experience. Anglo-Catholics often act like childish adults who are making a fuss over their environment. They do not like the Episcopal Church as it is, so they employ all their energies in making it something that it is not. A normally matured adult tries rather to adapt himself to reality. The Protestant Episcopal Church is a reality—quite wooden, stiff and conservative. The Roman Catholic Church is likewise a reality—always teaching dogmatically the old faith, but adapting herself slowly through the centuries to the changing needs of men. If one wants a refined, liturgical and socially irreproachable Protestantism, one can find it in the Protestant Episcopal Church. If one wants a developed and practical Catholicism, one can find it anywhere in the world in that vast ecclesiastical organization whose center is at Rome in the See of Peter.

The position therefore that I have maintained for many years, that it is God's will that I should do my small part in trying to Catholicize the Anglican Communion and thus bring her finally to reunite with the apostolic see of the West, seems to me now one that is tainted with pride and rendered futile by its childishness. Why did I not see this before? I do not know, unless it was because I did not want to run the risk of disturbing my emotionally comfortable state of life. It is alarmingly easy to deceive ourselves, and thus to remain convinced that our aims are irreproachable. May one not be permitted to grow wiser with advancing years?

III

Perhaps my change of heart may be explained in the terms of adaptation to environment. The conviction has been growing in me every year that I am in conflict with the prevailing trends of religion and thought in my environment. I am certainly out of sympathy with Liberal Protestantism, which is the dominant religious force outside the Church of Rome in that part of America in which my lot has been cast. Clergymen like Dr. Harry Emerson Fosdick, Dr. Robert Norwood, Dr. Walter Russell Bowie, Dr. Karl Reiland, Dr. Howard Chandler Robbins, Dr. Henry Sloane Coffin, Dr. S. Parkes Cadman, Dr. Howard Mellish, Bishop Lawrence, Bishop Slattery, Bishop Stires—to say nothing of the rich and influential laymen who stand behind them—undoubtedly represent the popular cast of religious thought and feeling in the social milieu with which I am familiar. They are all Liberal Protestants. My religious convictions have very little in common with theirs, although I have always found them delightful companions and courteously tolerant of my theological views. Fundamentalist Protestantism appeals to me even less than Liberal Protestantism. Anglo-Catholics represent but a tiny and almost negligible fraction of the forces of American Protestantism. They are commonly regarded as an eccentric, stubborn and amusing group that does not carry much weight in the ecclesiastical world.

My sympathies are with Catholicism rather than with Protestantism. The facts of contemporary religious life in America compel me to identify Catholicism with the Roman Catholic Church. The same facts force me to the conclusion that Protestantism is decadent and in process of dissolution. The Rev. Charles Stelze, speaking recently before one hundred ministers at the New York Advertising Club, declared that only six per cent of the population of New York City are members of the Protestant Church—whatever that is. He urged them to unite in advertising "the Church." He might better have advised them to try to come to some agreement as to what there is in Protestantism that is worth advertising. The Roman Catholic Church does not have to advertise, as its churches are filled to overflowing six or seven times every Sunday morning. Protestant Churches do advertise, and their congregations in the majority of cases are dwindling. No amount of advertising could sell a perfectly worthless food product to the American public. Let Protestant ministers advertise whatever it is that Protestantism has to offer the public that

Rome cannot offer. Perhaps they might agree on such features as free admission, services in English, eloquent and sensational sermons, extempore prayer by the minister, the absence of ceremonial, cushioned pews instead of hard kneeling-benches, dispensation from confession, freedom to believe as you like, beautiful anthems by the choir, the congregational singing of popular hymns, and so on.

It is plain that I am not in perfect *rapport* with my ecclesiastical environment. I recall reading an interesting article by Dr. Albert Jay Nock in *Harper's Magazine,* in which he attempted to explain the apparent discomfort of the average American business man while traveling in Europe, on the ground that the principles of mass production and salesmanship which dominate and control American civilization are not the dominant principles in Europe. A quite different spirit prevails there. "In consequence," says Dr. Nock, "when an individual passes from either civilization to the other, he is all the time played upon by spiritual ether-waves which powerfully affect his capacity for enjoyment."

It may be that the ether-waves of Protestant Liberalism are offensive to my Catholic convictions and sensibilities; or it may be that the ether-waves of an increasingly dominant Catholicism are exerting a

damaging effect on my one half of one per cent Protestant prejudices. Whichever is happening, it powerfully affects my capacity for enjoyment.

IV

One of my friends has tried to persuade me to
remain content with Anglicanism by the following
argument: "Everyone knows that Anglican ecclesiastical conditions are something of a mess. But they
are part of life, and all life is messy in this day and
generation. Some of us are fond enough of Anglicanism to bear with it; or we feel it is a better, because a more accustomed, natural way for us to
express ourselves spiritually; or we are so involved
in it through our responsibilities that we *cannot*
leave it. Do you or do you not think our orders are
valid, and our sacraments real sacraments? That
to my mind is the real question, and not the Papacy.
Given valid sacraments, we can live the Catholic
life, no matter whether we are in communion with
Rome and the Pope or not, and no matter how
shaky our ecclesiastical discipline, or how weak our
authority. Even in the lowest Protestant Episcopal
church—if we should be stuck in such a parish—
we could live the Catholic life if we could make our
communions. Would you be prepared to say that

you had never celebrated a real Mass or given a real absolution?"

In answer to this plausible presentation of the Anglican position, I should say that it is quite possible that we have valid orders and that our sacraments are real. To me however the crux of the matter is the Papacy. Did our Lord create His Church, not only with an apostolic ministry, but with one apostle, St. Peter, as the prince and leader of the apostolic college? If so, we must be in communion with the See of Peter. Dr. St. George, Professor of Ecclesiastical History at Nashotah House in Wisconsin, said in my hearing many years ago that it all hinged on the Papacy. If we believed in the Pope, we should become Roman Catholics; if we did not, we should remain Anglicans. There can be no doubt about the validity of the orders of the Eastern Orthodox Churches. The question at issue is whether they are justified in their separation from the apostolic see. That can be determined only by a study of the origins of the Eastern schism. To me the one question of importance is, what kind of Church did our Lord establish? I have no doubt that it was a Church in which the apostles were the chief ministers, and that the bishops of the primitive Church were the successors of the apostles. But that is not all. If any fact stands out strikingly in the Gospels and the Acts of the Apostles, it is that St. Peter was the chief of the apostles, and was so regarded by our Lord himself. If our Saviour was building his Church for all time, and not throwing together simply a temporary expedient, the assumption is strong that the successors of St. Peter in the Roman See are by divine ordering the administrative heads of the Church. In that case, we have no more right to eliminate the Papacy from the constitution of the Catholic Church, than Protestants have had to discard the episcopate. I have never been impressed with the Anglican argument that the primacy and supremacy of the Pope are merely *de jure ecclesiastico,* and not *de jure divino,* because the Papal claims rest on our Lord's commission to St. Peter. But even if the powers of the Pope had been given him by the Church, rather than by our Lord, those who believe that the development of the Church is guided by the Holy Ghost would still have to accept the Papacy. Otherwise they would have to assume that the Holy Ghost misguided the Church for the first thousand years of her history.

Hitherto I have never been much troubled by the question of the validity of Anglican orders. Of course I should prefer to believe that my orders were valid; but as to the people to whom I have ministered, I have never doubted that the sacraments they have received in good faith, and their other acts of devotion, have been effectual means of grace to them. I could not believe that God would not give His grace to all who diligently seek Him, and conscientiously make use of the best means they know for coming into union with Him. That is why there have been godly and heroic souls, not only in every kind of Christianity—however heretical—but in every religion.

Another paragraph from the letter quoted above sums up the difficulty very well: "I can see that it is all much harder from the priest's point of view. I should never want to convert anyone to Anglo-Catholicism. Because I have been born in it, I want—at present—to go on in it; but I should not want to drag anyone else into an unsatisfactory religious situation. I should advise Roman Catholicism if they were attracted to Catholicism in some form. But of course that is just what priests have to do—convert people and keep the Church going."

Precisely. An Anglo-Catholic clergyman must try to convert people to Anglo-Catholicism. If he begins to feel that Anglo-Catholicism is losing ground in the Anglican Church, and is a negligible factor in the religious forces of the modern world, and there is increasing evidence in contemporary history that the Roman Catholic Church is the most vigorous and flourishing presentation of the religion of the Gospel, he is inevitably driven to the conclusion that he must make his submission to Rome.

The Protestant Episcopal Church, as I see it now, is a heterogeneous conglomeration of clergy and laity, each of whom is individualistic in his religious beliefs and practices. The "yardstick" by which their ecclesiastical status is to be measured is the degree of their approximation to the religion of Rome. Sooner or later everyone becomes dissatisfied with bare Episcopalianism and borrows—by whatever intermediary—some belief or practice from Roman Catholicism: lights, vestments, incense, reservation of the Sacrament, the sign of the cross, the bowing of the head at the Holy Name, genuflections, the invocation of saints, the Rosary, the Hail Mary, the Angelus, the Stations of the Cross, retreats, adoration, confession, communion in one kind, the Breviary offices, the Immaculate Conception, Transubstantiation, the Primacy of the Pope, Papal Infallibility. Some Anglicans accept all of them, others only a few of them. They are all at various stages on the road to Rome.

The case for Rome keeps coming back at us like a medicine ball. We may handle it successfully many times and hurl it away from us with determination. There may come a time when it bowls us over. Mr. G. K. Chesterton says somewhere that it has been the experience of many who have joined the Roman Catholic Church that they have first gone through many moments of disturbance, from which they emerged, satisfied to remain where they were; but one day the conviction of the truth of the Roman position became so overwhelming that they could not avoid making their submission. That has been largely my experience. Many a time in my ministry I have felt the attraction of Rome, but I soon got over it. Now it is different. This is no passing fancy. I have lost my heart!

Chapter V

BORROWING FROM A RICH NEIGHBOR

I

FOR many years I have been conscious that I have been leaning very heavily on the Roman Catholic Church. In my private devotional life I have used chiefly Roman Catholic books for my meditations, especially those by modern French spiritual writers. I have made it a practice to say the Day Offices from the Roman Breviary whenever I could; and have fallen back on the Prayer Book Offices of Morning and Evening Prayer only when pressed for time. The Prayer Book Offices have bored me; the Old Testament Lessons, especially, seemed to be selected with the least possible regard for devotional inspiration. The prayers I have used for preparation for Mass and for thanksgiving after Mass are mostly from Roman sources; likewise the *secreta* at Mass and the special Collects, Epistles and Gospels for days not commemorated in the Prayer Book. For extra-liturgical services I have borrowed from Rome the service of Benediction of the Blessed Sacrament, the Holy Rosary, the Litany of the Saints, and many other litanies, also Exposition and Processions of the Blessed Sacrament.

This has been no personal eccentricity of my own. This borrowing is practiced by Anglo-Catholic clergy and laity the world over. Most of the practices of the laity, including genuflecting, bowing the head, crossing themselves, receiving Holy Communion in one kind, taking the Host in the mouth, their method of observing days of fasting and abstinence, which differs radically from the meager directions in the Book of Common Prayer, the keeping of vigils, the form used in making sacramental confession: —these and many other matters are copied from practices and ceremonies which they have often observed in Roman Catholic churches. Take away everything Anglo-Catholics have borrowed from Rome, and their devotional life would be almost a blank. The clergy would not even know how to say Mass, for there are practically no ceremonial directions in the Prayer Book, and our seminaries do not consider such matters important enough to have a place in the curriculum. Perhaps it is just as well. When our General Convention or the legislative bodies of the English Church set forth anything new on rites and ceremonies, as in the method of reserving the Blessed Sacrament, they nearly always make a botch of it by disregarding all that the Church has learned through the centuries of her experience.

I have always maintained that there can be no objection to borrowing from Rome—or from Islam, for that matter—if the thing borrowed proved devotionally helpful. But what kind of a Church is it that always keeps her children in rags so that they must borrow all their good clothes from their neighbors? Where should we be if Rome failed us? Are we not under greater obligation to Rome than we are to the Anglican Church? What are we doing to show our appreciation of our generous neighbor besides deriding her for her superstitions and her obscurantism? If Rome does so much for our devotional life and the *Ecclesia Anglicana* so little, is it not a reasonable inference that our place is in the Roman Church? "Catholicism without the Pope" may sound well in an argument with Protestants; but it is Catholicism with the Pope that keeps us from spiritual starvation.

II

There are not a few High Churchman, like the late Bishop Hall, of Vermont, who vigorously denounce all these borrowings from Rome as acts of disloyalty to the formularies as well as to the spirit of the Anglican tradition. Naturally, Churchmen of the Evangelical and Liberal schools denounce them even more vehemently. It must in all candor be admitted that there is something to be said for these denunciations of Anglo-Catholics. If the Church of England at the Reformation deliberately made certain departures from the Roman Catholic system, such as giving communion in both kinds, eliminating the invocation of saints, abolishing the Reservation of the Sacrament, and rejecting the supremacy of the Pope, it is questionable, to say the least, whether Anglo-Catholics have a moral or legal right to undo these changes and return to the *status quo ante*—merely on their own authority.

It is certainly true that the practice of reserving the Blessed Sacrament was discontinued in England for three centuries after the Reformation, and has been revived only in the past sixty years by the more advanced followers of the Oxford Movement. This revival of a pre-Reformation practice may have been justified by the necessities of pastoral work; but it has been carried through without the authorization of the legislative bodies of the Church. This is proved by the definite provision for Reservation in the revised English Prayer Book, which had so much to do with its being rejected by the House of Commons. Those who have been instrumental in reviving the practice of Reservation in the Church of England have fully realized that they were thereby undoing the work of the Reformation; indeed, they have for the most part gloried in the fact. But have they the right, merely on their own authority, to undo the work of the Reformation? I confess that I could not help feeling that there was some justification for the contention made by Lord Cushenden in the *London Times* of July 19, 1929:

Sir,—Archdeacon Hoskyns does not quote me accurately. I did not say that there was any "one single passage in the Revised Prayer Book" which teaches a form of faith repudiated for more than three centuries. What I do say is that it removes a prohibition against such teaching, thereby legalizing it (if the Book itself were legal) when given by the clergy. For more than three centuries the practice of Reservation has been prohibited—as it still is—in the Church of England, involving repudiation of the sacramental doctrine implied by that practice. There has of course been endless controversy as to the varieties of sacramental doctrine permissible to be held in the English Church, and the Archdeacon would probably deny that the prohibition of Reservation carried with it the repudiation of any form of faith. If so, he is entitled to his opinion, but I do not think it is shared, or ever has been, by the laity at large. I maintain that the illegal sanction of Reservation by the Bishops, whether in pursuance of the Revised Prayer Book, or otherwise, opens the door to the teaching of doctrines which it was one of the chief aims of the Reformers to repudiate and condemn.

I have never understood how it is possible adequately to minister in a large city parish without having the Sacrament perpetually reserved for the communion of the sick and dying, and of others who can never be present when the Eucharist is celebrated. That, however, is not the question at issue, which is simply whether the Anglican Church, since the Reformation, has authorized or forbidden Reservation. The rubric in the Prayer Book, which declares that none of the consecrated Bread and Wine should be carried out of the church, seems on the face of it, to forbid Reservation. I have come to feel strongly that I do not wish to belong to a Church which for more than three centuries has been so short-sighted as to fail to provide in an effective way for the communion of the sick and dying, especially in view of the fact that the Roman Catholic and Orthodox Churches of the East have always made such provision. The Church which properly looks after her children is the Church for me.

III

It is not only in my private devotional life and my public devotional practice that I have derived support and inspiration from the Roman Catholic Church, but also in my teachings of morals, and the counsel I give to penitents. In such matters as these, if the Anglican clergy could not rely on Rome, they would be in a worse plight than the Israelites when commanded to make bricks without straw. As a result of the emphasis made by the Continental Reformers on justification by faith only, Continental Protestantism has produced almost no systematic treatise on moral theology or casuistry. Why worry about conduct, when faith alone is sufficient? The Church of England seems to have been laid waste by the same blight, and only recently has any earnest effort been made to remedy her plight. Even so, the books that have been produced in the last few years by Anglican scholars on moral theology are largely compilations from Roman Catholic sources. Whenever they do depart from the authoritative Roman Catholic teaching on such subjects as Marriage, Contraceptive Practices, Divorce, Fasting, Obedience to the civil law, their opinions vary; consequently their readers are left in doubt as to the explicit teaching of the Church.

There are few Anglican confessors of any experience who do not rely mainly on Roman Catholic treatises on casuistry in solving the difficult moral problems that are presented to them in the confessional. What else can they do? Roman Catholic moral theologians are the only ones who cover the whole ground and speak with authority. One may be certain that they have behind them the authoritative rulings of the Church. It would be difficult to get any synod or convention in the Anglican Church to enunciate positive rulings on any question of morals. They would probably appoint a commission representing all schools of Churchmanship, which would meet at quarterly intervals for three or four years, and finally publish an elaborate report on the whole subject, with several alternative conclusions as to what the Church teaches. The long-suffering laity would wait patiently for their decisions, and when it came they would be as much in the dark as ever. The Anglican laity look to their spiritual leaders for guidance, and do not receive it.

When married people put to me the question, "Just what does the Church teach on the subject of birth-control?" I heave an inward sigh. I know that the Anglican Church teaches nothing on the subject, and that whatever answer I may give them, they can go to another Episcopal clergyman around the corner and get a different answer. All I can say to them is that it is the unanimous opinion of Catholic moralists that contraceptive practices are sinful. If they ask me whether I refer to Roman Catholic theologians, I must reply that they are the only ones who are teaching, not their own opinions, but the definite pronouncements of the Church. The Roman Catholic Church considers the subject of sufficient importance to teach courageously and decisively what is the moral duty of married people in the procreation of children. The Anglican Church knows that it is an important subject and appoints commissions to produce long reports which nobody will read. I shall be told that there are many Roman Catholics who are limiting their families by the use of contraceptives. This does not prove anything, for no doubt there are bad Catholics, and the fact remains that the Church continues to teach that they are committing sin.

Likewise many difficult questions arise relating to marriage and divorce. The Anglican Church has only one law on the subject—no remarriage of divorced persons. In the United States the exception is made that the innocent party in a divorce for adultery may marry again. There is no recognition of the Pauline privilege, which permits a Christian believer to remarry, if forsaken by an unbelieving wife or husband. There is no provision in Anglican canon law for a separation when the marriage was null and void from the beginning, even when it was never consummated. The Roman Catholic Church, on the other hand, bases her canon law on the clear-cut teaching that marriage is a sacrament, the voluntary union of a baptized man and a baptized woman, solemnized by a priest who has jurisdiction. She has specified a dozen or more diriment impediments which render the supposed marriage null and void *ab initio*. She never allows divorce. If the marriage fulfills all the canonical requirements, the man and woman are indissolubly bound together by a spiritual tie until separated by death. Any Roman Catholic who marries knows perfectly well whether he has the sanction of the Church. If separation is granted by the Church, on the ground of diriment impediments, a decree of annulment is issued, and both parties know that another union may be entered into without sin. Every experienced Anglican pastor knows of many cases where separations should be granted because there never was a real marriage; but he is powerless to act because of the inadequate canon law which stands in the way, although he knows that in the Roman Catholic Church a decree of annulment would be possible.

There is no subject upon which modern Christians are in greater need of guidance from the Church than the subject of morals. Many of them live among people who have definitely abandoned the moral standards of the Gospel. A generation ago, though many educated people had ceased to believe any longer in the dogmas of the Christian faith, they still paid conventional homage to the principles of Christian morality. Now, however, for those who imagine that the foundations of Christian dogma have been demolished by scientific rationalism, the superstructure of Christian morals has completely collapsed. Modern intellectuals are hopelessly confused in their efforts to build up any coherent moral system to take its place. Of course, the unbelieving modern world cannot be expected to give heed to the moral teachings of the Church; but the faithful have a right to demand from the Church inspired leadership and positive declarations on the vexing moral problems which they are compelled to meet in their daily life. It cannot be denied that the Roman Catholic Church is the only form of Christianity which professes to give her children infallible guidance as to how they should act. She teaches them with no uncertain voice what they must believe and do in order to be saved.

In the recent *Memoir* of Alice Meynell, her daughter points out that it was not sentiment or emotion or aesthetic appeal that led her mother to the Roman Catholic Church, but rather because she saw in that Church the logical administration of the Christian moral law (p. 42). Writing to her daughter Olivia, Mrs. Meynell makes the following statement, which is well worth quoting:

I saw, when I was very young, that a guide in morals was even more necessary than a guide in faith. It was for this I joined the Church. Other Christian societies may legislate, but the Church *administers* legislation. Thus she is practically indispensable. I may say that I hold the administration of morals to be of such vital importance that for its sake I accepted, and now accept, dogma in matters of faith—to the last letter. To make my preachment clearer: Right or Wrong (morals) are the most important, or the only important things men know or can know. Everything depends on them. Christian morality is infinitely the greatest of moralities. This we know by our own sense and intellect, without other guidance. The Church administers that morality, as no other sect does or can do, by means of moral theology. The world is far from living up to that ideal, but it is the only ideal worth living up to.

IV

In the realm of belief and dogmatic definitions of the faith, we are likewise compelled to fall back on

Rome for our authority, as well as for an intelligible exposition of the meaning of the articles of the creed, and of other elements of our religion not contained in the creed. What would have happened to the Catholic faith had it not been for the unflinching adherence and testimony of the Roman See to that faith through the ages?

If it were not for the knowledge that Rome stands impregnable in the background, Anglo-Catholics would often have grave fears for the future of the Catholic faith. The teaching of the Anglican bishops and parish clergy is often muffled and uncertain, and it is not unusual to find them differing radically in their interpretation of the creeds. Not a few of them attempt to explain away the articles in the creed, the articles which refer to the Virgin Birth and the Bodily Resurrection of our Lord, thus indicating that they do not hold the Catholic doctrine of the Incarnation. A still larger proportion of them repudiate the traditional Catholic teaching on the sacraments. They believe in the real absence of the Lord in the Eucharist rather than his Real Presence. They would not know how to hear confessions, even if they were willing. Is it any wonder that the laity are confused and do not know what to believe? We may tell them that the Prayer Book teaches the Catholic faith and provides for the administration of the Catholic sacraments. Next summer they may be told from an Anglican pulpit at the seashore that the Prayer Book does nothing of the kind, and that various interpretations are put upon it by different clergy. They do not need to be told that; actions speak louder than words.

When we want clear and concise statements as to what is of faith and what is permissible as of private opinion, we consult Roman Catholic books on dogmatic theology. The best Anglican dogmatic treatises do not differ from them very widely, except on some controverted points like the Immaculate Conception of Mary or Papal Infallibility. All our most trustworthy theologians would be only too willing to admit their indebtedness to St. Thomas Aquinas, and other more recent authorities on dogmatic theology in the Roman Church. Perhaps the best motto for Anglo-Catholics would be, "Look unto the Rock whence ye were hewn." In the field of dogma, as in the field of morals, we can pursue no other course. One would have to search a long time to find any dogmatic decisions of the Anglican Church written since the Thirty-Nine Articles. These Articles are intentionally ambiguous, and nobody knows what they really mean. The modern Anglo-Catholic must either accept the interpretation of Scripture as given by the best Anglo-Catholic scholars in such a book as the *New Commentary on Holy Scripture*, or he must rely on the dogmatic teaching of the Roman Church. The Anglican Church never teaches dogmatically.

they alone teach the orthodox faith. They also make the bold assertion that the Roman Catholic Church, spread throughout the world, teaching everywhere the same faith, offering the same Sacrifice, and exercising the same discipline, has added to or distorted the pure religion of the Gospel. As a working hypothesis this assumption of Anglo-Catholic infallibility demands a superhuman act of faith. One can imagine Job saying to the Anglo-Catholics of today, "No doubt but ye are the people, and wisdom shall die with you."

It is surprisingly easy to close our eyes to the facts! In every Anglo-Catholic parish which I have known the proportion of communicants who make their confessions regularly or their communions frequently, is lamentably small. They are but a handful of devout people, while the bulk of the parishioners feel that they have fulfilled their duty if they attend the late Eucharist on Sundays and listen to a sermon. Many a rector thinks he has a Catholic parish when only a dozen or more come out early on Sunday morning to make their communions, while the rest of his parishioners are satisfied with attending Matins at eleven o'clock. However large a number of parishes in England and America may have the outward insignia of Catholicism and be ministered to by Catholic-minded vicars or rectors, the number

of practicing Catholics among the laity is extremely
small. When the revised Prayer Book was debated
in the House of Commons the Anglo-Catholic position was not even stated, because there was no
Anglo-Catholic in the Lower House. In the General Convention of the American Episcopal Church,
there are almost no outspoken Anglo-Catholics
among the lay deputies.

It may fairly be said, therefore, that Anglo-
Catholics do not represent the prevailing sentiment
in any section of the Anglican Communion. This
became abundantly evident in the Malines Conver-
sations, which were conducted under the leadership
of Cardinal Mercier. These Conferences between
representatives of the Roman Catholic Church and
the Church of England were of undoubted value in
bringing out the points of difference between Roman Catholic and Anglo-Catholic theologians. The
storm that they raised in England was sufficient evidence that these Anglo-Catholic theologians did
not fairly represent the English Church. It would
have been the acme of unreality to suppose that
such conferences could have brought about the
reunion of the Church of England with Rome. Even
if the Church of England were one-quarter Anglo-
Catholic—which is very far from being the case—
it would be impossible to induce the overwhelming

matters that are unessential is certainly to exalt the Protestant principle of private judgment and do violence to the Catholic principle of authority.

That the whole question of obedience on the part of the clergy in the Church of England is at present very complicated, and that congregationalism largely prevails, is evident from the following letter to the *London Times*:—

There will be many of your readers who will be sorely perplexed by the decision of the bishops, just because there is no definite decision. How can the clergy obey a disunited episcopacy? This has been their difficulty all along. What will be permitted in one diocese is not to be permitted in another. The Bishops of London, Southwark, and Truro, and many others, will permit the use of the 1928 Book, and also Reservation, but the Bishops of Birmingham and Exeter and others are refusing to institute men to livings unless they promise not to reserve. There is no appeal, and the will or wish of the Parochial Council has just been flouted by the Bishop of Birmingham. Unless the bishops can agree to abide by a united policy, how can the Church of England cease to be congregationalist in practice, and how can the clergy expect to be obedient? This point of view should be most carefully studied by the laity.

Yours faithfully,
Wilfrid Hannay Gibbons, Rector of Oxted.

III

Thus it is extremely difficult to make out a logical case for Anglo-Catholicism. The whole position of Anglo-Catholics is grounded in disobedience, whether to lawful Anglican authority or to the authority of the Pope. The Anglo-Catholic claims to be subject to the authority of the whole Catholic Church, by which he must mean the Church of Rome, the Orthodox East and the various national Churches of the Anglican Communion. But how can Anglo-Catholics be said to submit to the authority of this vague ecclesiastical entity which they call the Catholic Church when they do not respect or obey the rulings of any of its component parts? The Anglo-Catholic is like a man who claims to be a citizen of the world, but refuses to pay taxes or join the army or obey the laws in any one country of the world. His cosmopolitanism and internationalism may be very beautiful sentiments; but they would not enable him to hold property or give him legal protection or carry him across any national boundary.

If a man wishes to belong to the Protestant Episcopal Church or the Church of England he should "play the game," submit to the lawful ecclesiastical authorities under whom he has enlisted, and practice the Christian religion as his Church has received the same. He may try to justify his eccentricities and acts of disobedience by talking about "immemorial Catholic precedent," "ancient and Catholic usage," or "the higher authority of the Church Catholic." He is appealing to something that does not exist, except in archaeological remains. The only place where he can find Catholic authority expressing itself today intelligibly is in the Roman Catholic Church. The Anglo-Catholic knows this perfectly well, and in his methods of reserving the Sacrament, celebrating Mass, giving counsel in confession, as in a hundred other matters, he relies on the living usage of Rome. He does not plunge into an historical investigation to discover how the Blessed Sacrament was reserved in the undivided Church of the eleventh century. He avoids that by consulting the directions of the Roman Congregation of Rites. Why then does he not say so frankly? A priest of the Russian Church does not adopt Roman Catholic practices and defend himself by the pretext that he is obeying "the higher authority of the Church Catholic." He obeys the canons, and submits to the bishops of the Russian Church. Orthodox authority is good enough for him. Why should not a priest of the Church of England teach the faith and administer the sacraments and discipline of his Church as the constitutions and canons and Prayer Book require, and as he has pledged himself to do by his oath of canonical obedience? Can it be that there is no Anglican authority that tells him in explicit terms how to perform the duties of his pastoral office?

Here again we are compelled to face the question of authority in the Church. An Orthodox Christian must submit to the authority of the Orthodox Church; a Roman Catholic is bound by the decisions of the Pope, the bishops and the conciliar decrees of his Church; the Anglican, whether he calls himself Anglo-Catholic, Modernist or Liberal Evangelical, certainly ought to obey the Prayer Book, the bishops, and the canon law of the national Church to which he has given his allegiance, whether English, Scottish, South African or American. A priest or layman in the Protestant Episcopal Church would have no right to flout the legislative enactments of General Convention and claim that he prefers to be guided by the canon law of the Church of England. How, then, can he have the right to accept only what has been decreed by the authority of Rome, even if he insists on calling it "the higher authority of the Church Catholic"? The most that he could do in this direction would be to follow the pre-Reformation beliefs and practices in matters which are not explicitly dealt with in the present formularies of his Church, as in the administration of the sacraments or the exercise of discipline.

I am driven logically to the conclusion that I must either be content with practicing and teaching the Christian religion as the American Prayer Book prescribes and "as this Church hath received the same," or—if that will not meet my devotional and doctrinal needs—join the Orthodox Eastern Church or the Church of Rome. As the Eastern Church is not for me a practical alternative, and I could never be spiritually content to return to bare Protestant Episcopalianism, the only intelligent course left for me is to submit to the Pope.

IV

But, it will be asked, how can you submit to the Pope in this age of democracy, in view of the fact that the democratic elements which were part of the constitution of the early Church have been, in the course of the centuries, completely nullified by the Papacy? Why not continue to protest against Papal assumptions until "government by the consent of the governed" shall once more have its place in the constitution of the Catholic Church?

I am willing to trust to the wisdom of the Catholic Church in dealing with democratic tendencies within the Church. If the Church has seen fit to centralize in Rome all ecclesiastical power and authority—although such is very far from being the case today—I can well believe that it is due to the firm guidance of the Holy Spirit. I am not convinced that democracy represents the fullness of governmental wisdom. It may be that it is only a passing phase in social evolution. In this so-called democratic age, there is a growing tendency among nations to put limitations on the rule of the people, and to resort to autocratic methods of government. Future developments may demonstrate that the Catholic Church was wise before the time in gradually eliminating many democratic elements which had a place in the government of the early Church.

Certainly in the Protestant Episcopal Church we have had abundant opportunity to test the value of lay representation in the councils of the Church. General Convention has supplied many lamentable exhibitions of theological incompetence and bigoted prejudice on the part of the lay deputies, resulting in the defeat of needed liturgical reforms and canonical revision. It was not an edifying spectacle in a recent Convention when an eminent lawyer satirized some of the most honored saints in the Church's history in his determination to prevent their being commemorated in the revised calendar of holy days. In the Church of England no changes in the worship of any parish church can be made without the consent of the Parochial Church Council, made up entirely of laymen. Lay representation in the governing bodies of the Church has resulted in a situation almost everywhere in the Anglican Communion which practically amounts to domination by the laity. This is quite different from the Catholic principle that all authority in the Church proceeds from Christ and works downward through the apostolic ministry to the laity.

The vestry system, which prevails in the Protestant Episcopal Church, is another illustration of government by the laity. The rector of a parish is supposed to be supreme in things spiritual, while the lay members of the vestry look after its temporal welfare. As the appointment of the rector rests with the vestrymen and they hold the purse strings, they really have the determining voice in regulating the conduct of the services, the ornaments of the church, and even the preaching in the pulpit. Other rich contributors who are not on the vestry often threaten to withdraw their support unless the rector makes certain changes in the ceremonial, or refrains from preaching doctrines which they do not like. This is intolerable to any clergyman who believes he has a commission from God.

In calling a rector, the wardens and vestrymen often consider a man's social standing, his ability to raise money, and even his rating as a golfer, rather than his spiritual gifts, his pastoral qualifications or his priestly experience and wisdom. Thus it often happens that clergymen with social influence and possessing worldly qualities which appeal to business men will receive the nomination to a rectorship, while men who are best qualified to be spiritual leaders will be passed by. Parishes would be more effectively administered if the appointment of rectors were in the hands of the bishop, as he is in a better position to understand the needs of the parish, as well as to know the character of the clergy and their spiritual competence.

If we believe that Christ gave full authority to St. Peter and the other apostles, and through them to the successor of St. Peter and the bishops in communion with him, to regulate the affairs of the Church, then we may safely leave all administrative matters to the rulers of the Church. They may move more slowly than we should like; but the Catholic Church thinks in centuries, and is wiser than the wisdom of any age. Submission to authority necessarily requires the curbing of the impetuous judgment of the individual. Conditions will not always be satisfactory to us and perhaps we are not always infallible in our prescriptions and demands. If the Holy Spirit is guiding the Church we can afford to wait for the correction of abuses.

If, on the other hand, we believe that the authoritative teaching of the Catholic Church can only be determined in the future, that it is being slowly worked out through what proves acceptable to the laity as well as to the bishops and other clergy, then we must be content with a perpetual flux of teaching and practice, and each member of the Church must fight for his own convictions. In this free-for-all fight the victory will be now with one side, and now with another. Only our children will know where the ultimate victory will lie. According to this pragmatic view of religious truth, the Church Militant here on earth is indeed a fighting Church; only we are engaged in a deadly conflict not so much with the world, the flesh and the devil, as with each other. This is a view of authority that commends itself to the intellectually proud and to all who love a fight. It is not so easy to reconcile with the divine teaching that we should love one another, or with the apostolic command to obey those who have the rule over us, and who watch over our souls as those who must give an account to God.

Chapter VII

HUMAN—ALL TOO HUMAN

I

THE Holy Catholic Church has her human side, and therefore we need not be surprised to find in her all the human frailties, inefficiencies, failures and sins. But she is also a divine organism, animated and directed by the Holy Spirit. Because of this supernatural power working within her the weaknesses and mistakes of men are overruled for good, sinful human agents become the instruments of sanctifying grace, and the human element in the ecclesiastical organism is transfigured by the divine.

After long observation of the practical workings of the Anglican Church, and comparing them with the everyday manifestations of Roman Catholicism, I am forced to the conclusion that in the Anglican system the divine element is almost swallowed up by the human. The human qualities in the Anglican clergy ordinarily determine the success or failure of their ministerial work, rather than the spiritual

gifts that they have supposedly received at their ordination. The social reputation of the parish, its
historical importance, its music or ceremonial, are
the factors that give it a temporary luster and enable it to prosper financially. In New York and
other large cities there are a few outstanding
preachers in the Episcopal Church, as there are in
the non-episcopal Churches, who attract large congregations. Other preachers, who are less eloquent,
sensational or heretical, hold forth to dwindling
congregations. Heresy, especially, has an extraordinary drawing power. People love to listen to a brilliant preacher who treats the historic creeds of the
Church as childish prattle of a bygone age, and fearlessly proclaims his own opinions and discoveries as
the new gospel for forward-looking, modern men.
Let the bishop interfere with him if he dares! His is
the church where one finds the crowds as thick as
flies on fly-paper.

Yet other Episcopal churches are presumably ad-
ministering the life-giving sacraments, preaching
the gospel of Christ, teaching the Catholic faith.
Their clergy are often men of real piety and consecrated life. They preach not themselves, but Jesus
Christ, and themselves the servants of their people for his sake. Why are their pews empty and
their altars deserted? Why must they be always beg-

ging for money to keep their churches open? I often wonder why more of them do not give up the ministry. Perhaps in this new day of talkies and television the Episcopal Church will be able to dispense with the services of several thousand of her clergy, and employ the radio to broadcast the much-lauded sermons of the metropolis to every town, village and hamlet in the land. Then every congregation could hear a soul-stirring sermon, and sing their favorite hymns every Sunday. That would satisfy the religious appetite of most church-goers—or perhaps it would not.

Even Anglo-Catholics tend to this adulation of the individual. They, too, have their favorite priests, to whom they flock for confession, and at whose "Masses" they prefer to communicate. They rightly esteem those who have devoted themselves wholeheartedly to God in the religious life. There are certain monastic preachers in England and America who always draw large congregations. Moreover, it often happens that a strong Catholic parochial work is built up by a particular priest, and when he dies or is transferred to another parish many of his followers find that they cannot practice their religion under his successor. This does not sound like the historic Christian religion. It is difficult to imagine the early Christians in a church in Asia Minor which had been established by St. Paul declaring that they could not go on because the parish no longer seemed the same after the great apostle had left. If the first Christians had been men of that sort there would probably be no Christian Church in the world today. They were devoted to the Church because it was the mystical Body of Christ, not because they liked Paul.

I look at the Roman Catholic Church today, and I find something that strongly resembles the religion of the early Christians. I see millions of people going to Mass every Sunday and fulfilling their religious obligations, regardless of the personality of the preacher or the priest who is saying Mass. I see churches packed to the doors at six or seven different Masses on Sunday morning. In Europe I have gone to a ten o'clock Mass on Sunday—a low Mass with no sermon or music—and could not find a seat. I was only one of a hundred or more who stood throughout. In a small American village I find not a few cultivated people who are devoted adherents of their parish church, in spite of the fact that their pastor is an uncouth, ignorant priest—from the point of view of our American intellectuals—although burning with apostolic zeal. I ask myself how long he would last in the average small-town parish of the Episcopal Church. The explanation of it all is that Roman Catholics see in the Church a divine organism that mediates to them the life of Jesus Christ. They see in every priest, whatever his personal limitations, an *alter Christus,* who speaks to them with the authority of God.

II

I know the answer that would commonly be given: Roman Catholics are driven to Mass by fear. They have been taught from childhood that it is a mortal sin not to go to Mass on Sundays and holy days of obligation, and that if they die in a state of unforgiven mortal sin they will go to hell. Whatever the explanation, the fact remains that they do go to Mass. In contrast to this, Protestants in increasing numbers are devoting the entire Lord's Day to pleasure. In view of this fact, Protestant criticism of this Roman Catholic teaching does not come with very good grace. How do we know that this teaching is not right? Those who despise the Mass here on earth, who will have nothing to do with the worship of God, who prefer their own pleasure to communion with the Divine Saviour, would probably find the environment of hell much more to their liking than the environment of heaven. They would be extremely uncomfortable before the throne of God, and would not greatly relish the companionship of the saints.

I do not wish, however, to be understood as blaming the Anglican clergy or laity because personal devotion to the clergy is the chief tie that binds the latter to the Church, rather than the ties of supernatural love and faith. It is not the clergy or laity, but the Anglican ecclesiastical system that is primarily responsible for this widely prevalent condition. The Anglican Church is "human—all too human." The Roman Catholic system, on the other hand, bears the marks of being sustained and permeated by the Divine Life. It is not its human elements that make it go. The outstanding spiritual wonder in modern Christendom is the sight of countless millions of people, many of them simple and ignorant, crowding the altars of the Roman Church, not only on Sunday, but every day in the week, to take their part in the sacred Mysteries, in spite of the fact that the Liturgy is rendered in the Latin tongue, which they cannot understand, and in a low voice, or whisper, which they cannot hear. This is a supernatural phenomenon which cannot be ignored.

The conviction has been growing stronger in my mind every year that in the Anglican Church too much depends on the human element, and too little on the divine. To make his parish a success an Anglican clergyman must be an indefatigable pastor, a good mixer, an interesting preacher, an efficient organizer, a clever financier, an up-to-date educator, a tireless letter-writer, a good story-teller, and a convivial companion at the dinner table. If all the graduates of her seminaries were only men of this calibre, the Protestant Episcopal Church would have a brilliant future. Today, however, most of our gifted young men become stock-brokers, bond-salesmen, bankers, capitalists and industrial organizers.

A man may be exceptionally gifted by nature, but he cannot accomplish as much for the Kingdom of God through his own natural talents as a less gifted man who has been ordained to the Catholic priesthood, and received the Holy Ghost for his office and work. Our Lord said that among all those who had been born of women there had not arisen a greater prophet than John the Baptist, but that the least in the Kingdom of God was greater than he. Those who have been ordained to the ministry of the Catholic Church, because of their sublime and intimate relationship with the Saviour, exercise a power that is of a totally different character from any power they would have through merely natural endowments. We see that power everywhere at work in the bishops, priests, missionaries and monks of the Roman Catholic Church. In the Anglican Church, and the great Protestant bodies as well, there are men of burning zeal and consecrated human gifts who, against overwhelming obstacles, do much noble work for souls. But the results are not the same.

A tree is known by its fruits. The actual character of the Anglican Church may be fairly inferred from the prevalent types of Anglicanism to be found in the men who hold the important positions in the Church, such as the majority of the bishops, the rectors of prominent parishes, and the leading laymen who represent their dioceses in General Convention. The Anglo-Catholic movement has been imposed upon the Anglican system like a transplanted vine, and does not flourish in its new environment. Anglo-Catholic types of piety are an artificial growth that does not strike down deep into the substance of Anglicanism itself. Anglo-Catholics are like foster-children that have been forced upon a family that does not really want them. The Episcopal Church in this country does not support Anglo-Catholic parishes and mission work as though she were proud of them, but only grudgingly and with much grumbling. The outstanding Anglo-Catholic diocese in this country at present is in a state of financial destitution and appealing for outside aid. Here and there are a few apparently flourishing Anglo-Catholic parishes, due to sporadic gifts from a few rich men. But the strong parishes in all our cities which are the natural outgrowth of the Episcopal Church, are of such character as to leave in no doubt the real ethos of Anglicanism.

It has often been argued by Anglo-Catholics that the Catholicity of the Anglican Communion is proved by the signs of Catholic life that still persist within her, such as Catholic devotions, the religious life, the practice of confession and attention to ceremonial. The signs of life, however, are not always indications of a vigorous life that will continue to grow. Practically everyone is familiar with what happens when the head of a chicken is severed from its body. The body for a time shows abundant signs of life, and is often quite as active as a chicken with a head. At the time of the Reformation the Church of England had its head cut off by Henry VIII, and signs of life have persisted even to our own time. But these signs now bear unmistakable evidence that the life is ebbing.

III

During my vacation in Europe in the summer of 1929, when I had abundant leisure to follow the ecclesiastical developments of the day, as reported in the public press, I could not help comparing the trend of events in the Roman Catholic Church as compared with the Anglican Church. The newspaper accounts of Roman Catholic activities impressed me because they demonstrated that this Church was always true to her principles and stood fearlessly for supernatural religion in the face of an unbelieving world. The utterances and actions of dignitaries of the Anglican Church did not impress me so favorably, because they seemed to be characterized by a worldly point of view—when not deliberately truckling to Protestant prejudice. They apparently shrank from setting forth boldly the supernatural claims of their Church, or from letting anyone suspect that they wished to be loyal to her Catholic heritage. To deal with this subject exhaustively would require volumes. I shall refer only to a few events which were reported in the *London Times*, which could certainly not be accused of being partial to the Church of Rome.

The splendid procession which took place in Rome on the occasion of the Pope's first appearance outside the Vatican for two generations, was one of the most moving historical scenes in my memory. I wish I might quote the whole of the admirable report in the *London Times* of July 26, 1929, but lack of space permits me only to touch upon it here and there. The procession was made to coincide with the visit of seminarians from all over the world to the Pope, on the occasion of his fiftieth anniversary of ordination to the priesthood. At six o'clock the head of the procession left the central doorway of St. Peter's and advanced slowly down the steps to the right leading into Bernini's vast colonnade. At seven-thirty the Pope appeared at the entrance to the Basilica, but owing to the length of the procession it was forty minutes before he left the *podium*. As he reached the foot of the altar the sight was one of unforgettable splendor. The altar had been placed in the center of the portico of St. Peter's, the columns of which were outlined by dimly burning lanterns. The broad steps were a shimmering sea of candles, from the midst of which came the sound of the massed choirs and the Papal band. A *Te Deum* was solemnly chanted. The silver trumpets gave the salute and a rustle was heard as the people knelt and the Italian troops presented arms. Slowly the Pope ascended the altar steps and gave Benediction to the kneeling multitude. Again the trumpets sounded, and the crowd rose to its feet. As the Pope began to move towards the Palace the pent-up feelings of the people were released in long and reiterated shouts of *Viva il Papa*. After the lapse of sixty years they could again welcome their Pope in their midst. The policing of the Piazza had been entrusted to the Italian government, and the task was fulfilled in a generous spirit by thousands of soldiers. The altar was made of bronze and marble, and was the gift of the late Cardinal Rampolla. A huge tapestry representing the Last Supper served as a reredos, and over it was a magnificent baldachin of red velvet and gold. The altar was decorated with beautiful silver candle-sticks of massive size. In the portico of the Basilica and round the colonnade were hung the famous Napoleonic tapestries presented by the Emperor Napoleon to Pope Pius VII after his coronation in Paris.

Moreover, I was filled with admiration for the ingenious counter-stroke of the Pope in his controversy with Mussolini on the subject of the Lateran Treaty and the Concordat. In this controversy the Pope had championed religious education as against secular, but Mussolini had forbidden the Catholic press of Italy to set forth the Papal views of the Treaty, while the secular Italian press had been given such permission. The Pope therefore took advantage of the occasion when five hundred seminarists from all over the world were in Rome to present to them a pamphlet containing all his utterances on the subject of the Concordat. In his address to the seminarists he hinted that they might translate his speeches into their respective languages, and thus publish his views to the whole world.

World-wide attention has been drawn to the dispute between Malta and the Vatican, over the fact that the government of Malta had interfered with the discipline of a Maltese friar by his ecclesiastical superior, an Italian. In this dispute the accusation was made that the government had instituted a reign of terror and that the Church had been openly insulted. It was contended by the Vatican authorities that the Church had no intention of interfering in political matters, but was merely trying to defend her liberties against secular interference. I cannot pass judgment on the details of this dispute. But I was interested to read in the *London Times* that the Papal Secretary of State, Cardinal Gasparri, wrote to the Bishops of Malta urging them to "continue with firmness coupled with the necessary prudence in the attitude hitherto adopted by them against certain members of the Maltese Cabinet who, while publicly professing themselves to be Catholics, follow a policy which is very harmful to religion and the Catholic traditions of the Maltese." This incident exemplifies the fearless attitude of the Roman Catholic Church toward worldly powers, which has found abundant expression everywhere in the modern world: in Italy, Russia, France, Czecho-Slovakia, Mexico and other countries.

In the course of these same few weeks I have been less edified by press reports of three ecclesiastical events in the Church of England: the Thanksgiving for the recovery of the King; the Archbishops' Pastoral Letter to the Church; and the Sunday service for the Boy Scouts' Jambouree. How much more fitting it would have been if the King had made his thanksgiving at a solemn Eucharist in Westminster Abbey. Instead of that, the thanksgiving was framed on the model of Matins to conform to the Protestant prejudices of the majority of Englishmen. There was, however, on the same day in Westminster Cathedral, a Pontifical High Mass of thanksgiving for the King's recovery, with the King of Spain present in the sanctuary. Could anything more clearly demonstrate the Protestant character of the English Establishment?

The Pastoral Letter of the two archbishops was an appeal to the clergy and laity of the Church of England to make a serious study of "the whole Gospel of God." Apparently the archbishops hoped in this way that the Church would come to some agreement as to what is the Christian faith, as if the primary function of the Church were not to teach the Christian faith. This is just the sort of vague episcopal pronouncement, in stilted and abstract language, with which Anglicans are only too familiar. Such pronouncements have not the slightest effect on the life of the Church, to say nothing of the world in general. The root of the trouble which so deeply concerns the archbishops is the fact that the children of the Church of England are not being given a religious education. In Great Britain, as in this country, Rome alone is meeting this need effectively. The great public schools of England, such as Eton and Harrow, which are training the leaders of the future, are certainly not giving any education in religion worthy of the name. Moreover, as the *Church Times* well says, in commenting on the Pastoral Letter, "if there is vagueness and uncertainty among our people, is it not largely due to the episcopal fondness for coquetting with Protestantism, Undenominationalism, and Liberalism?"

At the out-door religious service on Sunday for the Boy Scouts' Jambouree, which was presided over by the Archbishop of Canterbury, there was nothing distinctively churchy or sacramental. It was merely a union service of prayer and praise for the Boy Scouts who belonged to the Church of England and all the Protestant denominations. At the same hour, Cardinal Bourne presided over a solemn outdoor Mass for the Roman Catholic Scouts, and preached a sermon in which he urged the boys to be loyal to their Church and its worship wherever they were. Not a word in the sermon of the Archbishop of Canterbury or the service which he sanctioned would have led the boys present to suspect that the Church of England was anything more than one of the Protestant denominations.

The Church of England is dominated and its development determined by human respect. Loyalty to God and to the Catholic heritage of the Church are sadly lacking in her authorities. It is becoming increasingly evident that the disease of worldliness is slowly paralyzing the Anglican Communion.

Chapter VIII

THE SHADOW OF PETER

I

THUS far I have been trying to describe my reactions to Catholicism without the Pope. After a varied experience of thirty years in the ministry of the Protestant Episcopal Church, I am forced to the conclusion that Catholicism without the Pope, so far as I am concerned, has been weighed in the balances and found wanting.

But why not Catholicism with the Pope? Why this extraordinary antipathy to the most ancient and venerable of all institutions in the modern world? Any schoolboy could tell us that Catholicism without the Pope is a contradiction in terms. It is like speaking of Catholicism without confession, or Catholicism without the Mass. The only body of Christians in the world today that officially calls itself Catholic is that very considerable section of Christendom which is living under the Papal obedience. The Churches of the East call themselves Orthodox; to them a Catholic is one that is subject to the jurisdiction of the Pope. If any national group in the Anglican Communion began officially to call itself Catholic, it would result in a schism in that group. In ordinary modern speech everywhere a Catholic is a Roman Catholic. Anglicans who claim to be Catholic are reduced to the necessity of calling themselves Anglo-Catholics, if they wish to be understood; even then, it requires much explanation. I remember once, years ago, seeing a colleague of mine talking long and vociferously with an old lady and making many gestures. They were too far away for me to hear what they said. I asked someone why he was talking so long, and was told that he was trying to explain the Anglo-Catholic position to a deaf woman. I have often found it quite as difficult to expound the position to those who have ears to hear.

The Roman Catholic position is simple by comparison, and can be stated cogently even by the unlearned. One morning a rough-looking young fellow spoke to me at the church door, and asked what was the difference between our Church and the Roman Catholic. I answered that we did not accept the claims of the Pope to supreme jurisdiction over the whole Church. He then wanted to know how we interpreted Christ's words to St.

Peter, "On this rock I will build my Church, and the gates of hell shall not prevail against it." I was amazed at such an apt retort from a man who was apparently uneducated. I replied that many of the Fathers of the early Church interpreted the rock as referring to Peter's confession, "Thou art the Christ, the Son of the living God." He shook his head as he added, "But Christ said, Thou art Peter, and Peter means rock." As I left him I wondered how many Anglicans of his station could explain so concisely their ecclesiastical position.

The Papacy is the outstanding feature of the Catholic religion in our modern world. Everything the Pope says and does is front-page news everywhere. He is the mouthpiece of Christian idealism, the spokesman for Christian morality, the one universally recognized representative of the Christian Church. It is not merely because he is a temporal sovereign that almost every civilized nation sends a representative to the Vatican. That was equally true while the Pope was yet the "prisoner of the Vatican." The reason is that most nations feel that they must be in a position to treat officially with the head of so widespread and powerful an international organization as the Roman Catholic Church. Moreover, every visitor to the city of Rome, whatever his religion, makes every effort to arrange for an audience with the Pope. Foreign visitors hardly display the same eagerness for an audience with the Patriarch of Constantinople or the Archbishop of Canterbury.

It may be said in reply that this widespread prestige of the Pope is due to the universal habit of newspaper-reading and to the fact that everyone wants to see those who are talked about in the public press. But is it too much to believe that the divine foreknowledge took into consideration just such developments in this and in every age? One illustration of this is that the Catholic Church abolished the practice of communicating the laity from the chalice centuries before the abolition of the common drinking cup on hygienic grounds. Another instance is to be found in the effect of the radio on the Church. The radio has not decreased the attendance in Catholic churches as it has in Protestant churches, because every Catholic is under obligation to go to Mass on Sunday. On the other hand, the radio has brought Catholic music, devotions, sermons and answers to questions to millions of people who would never have entered a Catholic church. In the same way, the Papacy has proved itself perfectly adapted to an age in which the authoritative utterances of the chief representatives of any large society, corporation or government are broadcast to every hamlet and farmhouse, and may be read the next morning at the breakfast-table in every home.

Every human organization, whether political, industrial, commercial, financial or social, has its administrative head. Why should not the Church Militant here on earth likewise have an administrative head? The Church of England has her Primate; the Protestant Episcopal Church has found it necessary to elect a Presiding Bishop; why should not the Catholic Church have a Pope? If our Lord had founded his Church without making provision for such an administrative head, he would have founded a Church which was ill-adapted to succeed in a world where so much depends upon organization.

II

Professor Foakes Jackson's book, *Peter, Prince of Apostles,* is one of the most illuminating books I have read for a long time. I had never realized before the tremendous importance of St. Peter in the Gospels, the *Acts* and the subsequent history of the Church. Both in the synoptic tradition and in the fourth Gospel St. Peter is of far greater importance than all of the apostles together. He is always mentioned first in the lists of the Twelve, he is the first one to confess the messiahship and divinity of Jesus. He repeatedly acts as the spokesman of the apostles. There can be no doubt that our Lord regarded him as the chief apostle, and gave him the name, Peter, or *Cephas,* meaning rock, and that in consequence he was always known thereafter as Simon Peter. He was the first of the apostles to whom our Lord appeared after his resurrection, and to him was given the special commission, "Feed my sheep." Most important of all, perhaps, is the power of the keys that was given by our Lord to St. Peter. According to the account in St. Matthew, our Lord said to Peter, "I will give unto thee the keys of the kingdom of heaven: and whatsoever thou shalt bind on earth shall be bound in heaven; and whatsoever thou shalt loose on earth, shall be loosed in heaven." Canon Lacey, in his book, *Authority in the Church,* has this to say of the power of the keys:

The kingdom of heaven is, in Matthew, the regular denomination of the messianic dispensation. The gift of the keys is the investiture of the steward, or chief minister; the phrase recalls the 22nd Chapter of Isaiah, where Eliakim is substituted for Shebna, "The key of the House of David will I lay upon his shoulder." Binding and loosing are regular terms of legislative and judicial authority. The exercise of this power in heaven does not belong immediately to my subject, but the exercise of it on earth can mean nothing else but legislative and judicial authority in the Christian Church, the People of God. . . . It is the general sense of the whole passage that counts for value. The sense is that Peter is promised the charge of chief minister in the messianic kingdom, soon to be organized on earth. (P. 46.)

In the *Acts of the Apostles*, St. Peter likewise assumes a position of paramount importance. Dr. Foakes Jackson says, "There are in Westcott and Hort's edition of the New Testament, 1027 lines in the first twelve chapters of *Acts*: of these 622 relate what was done and said by Peter, including 197 devoted to the single episode of the conversion of Cornelius. That Peter is the spokesman of the Twelve and takes the lead on every occasion, is unquestionable." In the *Acts,* according to Dr. Foakes Jackson, there are two Peters, the Peter of the Gospel, and Peter, the head of the apostolic college. He means by this not that they are two distinct individuals, but that St. Peter has developed from the fisherman, as pictured in the Gospel—impulsive, affectionate, swift to act but often led into difficulty by his haste—into the more balanced and authoritative leader of the Church.

Dr. Foakes Jackson makes the interesting suggestion that when the *Acts of the Apostles* records

I say, that everyone of you saith, I am of Paul; and
I of Apollos; and I of Cephas; and I of Christ."
(I Cor. i: 12.) From this it appears that St. Peter
is known to the Corinthians as an authority in the
Church, and an authority who ranks above Paul
and Apollos. The only higher authority than that
of Peter is the authority of Christ.

In writing to the Corinthians St. Paul insists that
all of these leaders, whether himself, Apollos or
Cephas, are but servants of the servants of God;
and that all, apostles and the faithful, are Christ's
as Christ is God's. He never contests the privilege
accorded to St. Peter as having been the first to
whom the risen Lord showed himself. (I Cor.
xv: 5.) He puts St. Peter ahead of the other apostles, even the brethren of the Lord, when he says,
"Have we no right to lead about a wife that is a believer, as well as other apostles, and as the brethren
of the Lord, and Cephas?" (I Cor. ix: 5.) He
utters no word of criticism against the authority
which some of the Corinthians recognized in St.
Peter.[1]

IV

The second argument against the claim to supremacy is that the general consent of the Church

[1] *Batiffol: Catholicisme et le Papauté*, p. 28.

has always been lacking. In particular, it is alleged
that the Papal claims were never recognized in the
East. A great deal is made of a quotation from the
history of the Church by Duchesne, a Roman Catholic historian, Vol. II, pp. 659–661. In this passage
the historian is explaining how the authority of
the Emperor insinuated itself into Catholicism. He
says that the Christian religion in the fourth century became the religion of the Emperor, not only
in the sense that it was professed by him, but in
the sense that it was directed by him. And this
evolution was brought about because "the Papacy
as the West knew it later on was yet to be born."
In other words, there was not, in the Church of the
fourth century, "an authority central, recognized
and effective." Of course it is obvious that the
Papacy, as it later developed, did not yet exist
in the fourth century. It had not sufficient power
and prestige to assert itself effectively against the
imperial power. But no one who is familiar with
the facts of history can deny that there existed
in the Catholicism of the time of Theodosius a
Church which was a norm of authority, recognized
and consulted by all. The Roman Church was the
Church in communion with which it was necessary
to be if one were to belong to the *Ecclesia*. It was
the only Church in the world which pretended

to have a care for all the Churches. It was a Church which believed it had a right to welcome the bishops whom Eastern councils had deposed, to pronounce on their causes, and to send them back to their dioceses vindicated and strengthened. It was the Church to which the Orientals appealed as in the time of St. Basil, to determine for them the orthodoxy of doctrines or of persons.

This normal development of the apostolic see as the center of unity was interfered with in the East by the policy of Constantine, toward the end of his reign, and the subsequent policies of the Emperors Constance II and Valens. As a result there was imposed on Catholicism a Caesaro-Papism, against which the Catholicism of St. Athanasius and St. Hilary was a magnificent protest. This Caesaro-Papism was itself the product of Arianism in its efforts to revise the Nicene Creed. The East returned to the faith of Nicaea in the time of Theodosius, but never wholly threw off the shackles of temporal domination, which even to the present day has been the chief defect of Greek Catholicism. Western Catholicism, on the other hand, strengthened the ties which bound it to Rome. St. Ambrose of Milan helped greatly in this process by his doctrine of the independence and supremacy of the Christian ministry. Greek Catholicism and Western

Catholicism tended more and more to oppose each
other as two mentalities and two distinct methods
of government. The Roman Church sensed the
danger of this disunity and bent all her energies to
forward the cause of unity through the primacy
of the apostolic see. Unity and the primacy were
two values which she knew belonged to the past
of Catholicism. Duchesne, in his *Eglises Séparées,*
is worth quoting:

Thus all the Churches of the entire world, from
Arabia, Osroëne, Cappadocia, even to the extreme limits
of the West, felt in all things, in faith, in discipline, in
government, in ritual, in works of charity, the unceasing
action of the Roman Church. She was everywhere
known, as St. Irenaeus said, everywhere present, everywhere respected, everywhere followed in her direction.
As against her, there was no competition, no rival. No
one ever dreamed of putting himself on the same foot-
ing with her. Later on there will be patriarchates and
other local primacies. But in the course of the third
century we only just begin to see traces, more or less
vague. Above these organisms in process of formation,
as above all isolated Churches, the Roman Church lifts
herself in her sovereign majesty, the Roman Church
represented by her bishops, a long line which comes
down in succession from the two leaders of the apostolic
college, who feels herself, declares herself, and is considered by the whole world, as the center and organ of
unity.

Undoubtedly it is true that from the time of Constantine to the seventh ecumenical council (323–787) the Greek Church was often in schism from the Church of the West. The Orientals have always had a feeble sense of the unity of the Church. Their actions were often animated by a dislike of submitting to Western rule (somewhat, perhaps, as the industrial East feels toward the agricultural West in the United States), a dislike which the Emperor, ruling from Constantinople, often had political reasons for encouraging. For 203 out of the 464 years of this period the Eastern Bishops were in schism from the apostolic see. The grounds for these schisms will hardly bear examination. One schism was in defense of Arianism, another arose over the condemnation of Chrysostom, another was the schism of Acacia, another was in regard to Monotholitism, and another was on the worship of images. In all these instances the apostolic see was defending the orthodox faith!

It is argued by Anglo-Catholics that the general councils never consented to recognize any primacy in the Bishop of Rome except the same kind of primacy that they claimed for the Bishop of Constantinople. The 28th canon of Chalcedon enunciated this principle of equality between Constantinople and Rome, but Pope Leo the Great protested vigorously against this canon. The Emperor Marcian intervened and compelled Anatolius, the Bishop of Constantinople, who inspired this canon, to make amends to the Bishop of Rome and to obey the laws of the Church. Thereupon Anatolius wrote to Pope Leo that he had nothing to do with the passing of the canon, but that some of his clergy had drawn it up and the bishops had voted for it. He added that the confirmation of all the ... of the council was of course reserved to the Pope. These are his words: *Cum et sic gestorum vis omnis et confirmatio auctoritate vestrae beatitudinis fuerit reservata.* (Since the whole validity and confirmation of the acts of the council will be reserved to the authority of your Holiness.) This does not look like a "presidency of honor."

The consequence of the Council of Chalcedon is the termination of the schism of Acacia in 515, and the formulary which Pope Hormisdas imposed upon the bishops of the East for their signature before he admitted them to the communion of the Church. This formulary which was accepted by the Oriental episcopate professes that the Catholic faith has always been preserved unimpaired in the apostolic see, that the only valid communion is communion with this apostolic see, that whosoever is not in communion with the apostolic see is separated from the communion of the Catholic Church, and his name cannot be mentioned in the celebration of the Holy Mysteries.[1]

V

To one who believes that Almighty God has a regulating influence in the development of the human race, that whom He will He lifts up, and whom He will He casts down, the facts of history cannot but be of supreme importance. Although no final argument can be based upon the facts as they exist at any one time, yet it makes us wonder, when we look at the situation in the countries of the world today where the Eastern Church has been dominant. In Asia Minor, where the Churches established by St. Paul have persisted down to our own time, every trace of Christianity has now been wiped out by the Turks. In Russia, the Bolshevist Revolution has put the Church in captivity. In Palestine, the future of the Orthodox Church is very precarious. In none of the Balkan States can the outlook for the Orthodox Church be called hopeful. There is a constant struggle going on between the various States as to which will have control over

---

[1] In the above section I am indebted to Batiffol's argument in the book cited on p. 135.

the patriarch. Everywhere the Orthodox Church is reaping the rewards of its subservience to the temporal power in the past.[1]

The situation is strikingly different in those countries where the Roman Catholic Church is supreme, or where she occupies a strong position. In Italy, the long struggle with the Italian Government has reached an amicable settlement. In France, the religious orders are coming back and the Church is a power to be reckoned with. In Spain, the Church has once more been established. In Germany, all the developments since the War have resulted in greatly strengthening the position of Roman Catholicism. Even in England there has been a striking number of conversions to Rome. In Mexico the serious quarrel between the Church

[1] The rapid disintegration of this institution (Mt. Athos), which had weathered the tide of years and storms of circumstance so long, is only an especially striking symptom of the general slump of the Church under whose aegis it flourished. With the advent of Bolshevism in Russia, and the splitting up of Greek Orthodoxy into the national Balkan Churches, Orthodoxy lost much of its vitality and most of the 200,000,000 adherents it numbered fifty years ago. In Russia it may still have latent strength which cannot be gauged. In the Balkans it can now count, and that only in a strictly general sense, on perhaps 15,000,000 members. By admission of its own rulers it is passing through troublous days, whose outcome may well be union with Anglicanism or absorption into the Roman Catholic Church, after a 1,000-year-old schism. (From an article on the Monastery of Mt. Athos, in the *New York Times* of Jan. 5, 1930.)

and the State has come to an end and the Church is once more carrying on her work. Conditions ten years from now may be entirely different, but one cannot but be impressed to see how contemporary world movements are working out in favor of Catholicism.

It has often been said that the growth of the Papacy in the early centuries and later in the Middle Ages, was entirely due to its connection with the Empire and the importance of the city of Rome as a center of world rule. But this is an argument that can be used equally well in favor of the Papacy. May we not say that it was by the divine ordinance that the Papacy was established in the city of Rome, rather than in Constantinople or Jerusalem or Alexandria or Antioch, where it would later on be deprived of its power? Shall we call it simply a piece of good luck, or shall we ascribe it to the providence of God?

The alternative to believing that the Papacy is a part of the divine constitution of the Church is to believe that it has been foisted on the Church by the machinations of evil men and the fortuitous turn of historical events. If we accept the latter alternative, then we are forced to the conclusion that the greater part of the Catholic Church has fallen into error. This involves too much, for it means that the Holy Spirit has not been guiding the Church into all truth, and that our Lord was mistaken when he promised that the gates of hell should not prevail against his Church.

Chapter IX

THE PRIMACY OF PETER

I

HAVING arrived at this point in the writing of my book, I felt that it was not right for me to continue longer as Rector of St. Mary's. Therefore I contemplated resigning from the rectorship on October 1, 1929, to take effect November 1. Before taking such a step I thought it best to consult my old friend, Dr. Barry, and let him know in advance of my intentions. Toward the end of September I spent a day with him in Kingston. He was deeply disturbed by my announcement, and told me that if I carried out my purpose I would shake the faith of many and jeopardize the salvation of my own soul. Nevertheless, we discussed the whole Roman question amicably, but vehemently, for several hours. I felt that owing to the precarious condition of his health I ought not to burden him with it any further, so I returned to New York. A few days later I received from him the following letter, which I determined to make the basis for further historical study of the Papacy:

The two crucial points in regard to the modern theory of the Papacy are (1) *jure divino* jurisdiction, (2) infallibility.

If St. Peter was commissioned by our Lord to be the head of his Church with these powers, this fact must have been known from the beginning and have controlled the development of the Church.

As a matter of historical fact, there is no evidence that the development of the Church was so controlled.

The Roman theory is of purely Western development. The East was chiefly interested in speculation—thinking out the meaning of religion—hence was the sphere of controversies. The West was interested chiefly in matters of practical government.

Take four centuries—the time from the Reformation until now would be the equivalent—a time in which much can happen. What did not happen was that the Church was guided by the modern Roman theory.

Take St. Peter. After the first chapters of the Acts he fades out of the picture. He does not appear as Supreme Head, but as one of the apostles. St. Paul consults Peter, James and John. The "Council of Jerusalem" is a conference, not an assembly to listen to a *proprio motu* or a bull.

St. Paul takes the center of the stage. He says that
to him is committed the care of all the Churches. Think
what we should have been told about this if it had
been said by St. Peter: how the whole papal theory
would have been deduced from it, and we should have
been left speechless. But as St. Paul said it, we interpret
it quite naturally, without reading any later meanings
into it.

As to the Keys. The one meaning *not* given by the
early interpreters is the modern Roman one. The Rock
means all sorts of things to the Fathers. How could it,
if the Petrine claims were of divine institution? The
early writers most often—almost exclusively—speak of
the Roman See as founded by SS. Peter and Paul, not
exclusively by Peter.

The fact that there is no mention of any rule or special influence by St. Peter in the early writers, and that
this is evidence that the early writers knew of no
Petrine claims, is *not* an argument from silence. The
evidence is positive that the Church organization developed in a quite different way from what it would
have had the Petrine claims been recognized. Its organization was not developed under the direction of
Rome, nor was its conception of authority Roman; its
development was conciliar, its appeals were to the voice
of the episcopate.

It is true that leaders often appealed for the support
of Rome. But so they did for the support of Alexandria

or Constantinople. To beg for support in controversy is one thing, but appeal to a tribunal is another.

The Roman controversialist reads back into the chance utterance of the early writers the modern theory of the Papacy. If we had not the developed theory, no one would think of deducing it from passages quoted from Clement, Ignatius, etc.

Moreover, the Roman controversialist is constantly playing with words: jurisdiction, supremacy, primacy; not very honest jugglery.

The Western Church became utterly corrupt. Attempts for reform were all blocked by Rome. In the end the Reformers were read out of the Church. They did not intend to depart from the Church; they were driven out. They still claimed to be of the Church. Under the circumstances it was inevitable that they should go further than they had intended and produce sects. The responsibility is Roman mostly. It is a well-known maxim that he who claims more than is rightly his, loses what is rightly his. The Anglican Church declined to submit to unjust claims, and was therefore excommunicated by the Pope. It has been compelled to maintain the faith under very difficult circumstances, and it is no wonder that it has made mistakes.

You have a standard American mind. The American business man who has no religion says, if I ever join a Church, it will be Rome. Why? Because he conceives it as an efficient organization. (Which, by the way, it is not, and never has been; otherwise it would not have split the Christian world into flinders.)

You are looking at efficiency, centralization, standardization. You admire these as you admire a big business corporation or a sky-scraper. But the standardization of the Roman Catholic Church since Trent has been disastrous. Religion is not big business.

The above letter states concisely the traditional Anglican criticism of the Roman Catholic claims. It is a line of argument with which I have been long familiar, and have hitherto accepted without question. It was the writings of Anglican scholars that first helped me to detect its fallacies, especially Professor Cuthbert Turner's articles in *Theology*, Dr. Foakes Jackson's *Peter, Prince of the Apostles*, and Dr. Scott's *The Eastern Churches and the Papacy*. Various addresses of Lord Halifax had also helped to open my eyes.

II

One of the things that have become increasingly clear to me through my study of the New Testament, is that St. Peter was given by our Lord jurisdiction over the whole Church, as well as the promise that he would be infallibly guided in his decisions. One of the best treatments of the subject

that I have found is that of Professor Cuthbert
Turner in the August and October issues of
Theology for the year 1926. Professor Turner is
an Anglo-Catholic and holds the chair of Ireland
Professor of New Testament Exegesis in the University of Oxford. These two articles had greatly
disturbed me when I first read them in 1926. I
submitted them at that time to Dr. Barry, but
never could get a rebuttal from him. He was then
preparing a course of lectures on the Papal claims,
but for reasons of health they were never delivered.

Professor Turner makes it clear that the Gospel
of St. Mark, which reports the substance of St.
Peter's preaching, lays less stress than the other Gospels on the extraordinary powers of primacy and
jurisdiction conferred by our Lord on St. Peter.
He attributes this to St. Peter's humility. St. Peter
had learned the lesson from his Master that true
greatness was not to be found in exercising lordship
over his brethren, but in being the servant of all.
Of the Gospel of St. Mark Professor Turner says
that, like the others, it marks out Peter as the
leader and spokesman of the disciples, and later
observes that none of the other Gospels adds anything to our knowledge of St. Peter, save in the
direction of confirmation of his preëminence as
leader among the disciples of Christ.

The other three Gospels, however, St. Matthew, St. Luke and St. John, which represent the Jewish, the Pauline and the Johannine tradition, record the three great sayings of Christ to St. Peter, which established him in his position of leadership in the apostolic Church. St. Matthew gives us the famous incident of St. Peter being called the Rock on which the Church was to be built, and being entrusted with the power of the keys; St. Luke the promise that his faith would not fail, and that after his conversion his task would be to confirm or strengthen his brethren; and St. John the commission to feed the whole flock of Christ: "Feed my lambs . . . rule my sheep . . . feed my little sheep." [1] It is difficult to see how the gift of jurisdiction by divine right and the gift of infallibility could be more clearly expressed. Dealing with the four Gospels as a whole, Professor Turner says:

What impresses me more than anything else is the convergence of the testimony of these four documents in the prerogative position allotted to St. Peter. The writers are not simply repeating one another; the more important sayings are different, the indications to all appearances independent; but they cohere to a remarkable degree, and they must, I think, be taken to represent the common attitude of all parts and sections of the Christian society in its earliest stages.

[1] The translation of this passage is that given by Professor Turner.

I will now take up these three great Petrine passages from St. Matthew, St. Luke and St. John, and inquire whether they are to be interpreted as implying that our Lord gave to St. Peter jurisdiction over the whole Church, and infallibility in his decisions.

It is often urged by Anglican controversialists that the majority of the Fathers interpreted the Rock (St. Matt. xvi: 18) to mean St. Peter's confession rather than St. Peter himself. The truth is that the early Fathers, as was customary among Greek commentators, interpreted the rock to mean a number of things: St. Peter, St. Peter confessing, his confession that Christ was the Son of the Living God, and even Christ himself. But it would be difficult to find any of the early Fathers who did not at some time interpret the rock to mean St. Peter. Certainly, this is the interpretation of the best modern commentators. The *New Commentary* on the Bible edited by Bishop Gore points out that the Greek of this passage means "Thou art *Petros* (stone) and on this *Petra* (rock) I will build my Church," and goes on to say that Jewish parallels "make it clear that the rock on which the Church is to rise is Peter himself and not our Lord." But, according to this commentator, Peter is Peter only by the faith that makes him what he is, and the promise therefore is only a personal promise. I will later come to the question as to whether this promise was interpreted by the Church to apply to St. Peter's successors also. The point I now wish to emphasize is that to interpret Peter as the rock on which Christ built his Church is in harmony with the best modern scholarship. Even Bishop Gore in *The Holy Spirit and the Church* (p. 48, footnote 2), says "The rock is surely the person" (of Peter). The *New Commentary* also interprets the power of the keys (vs. 19) conferred upon St. Peter as follows: "So the meaning of verse 19 is that Peter, as an administrator of the Kingdom of Heaven, will have a divinely recognized authority to teach and discipline the future community." This certainly implies *jure divino* jurisdiction over the whole Church.

The passage from St. Luke (Ch. xxii: 31–32) may best be translated as follows: "Simon, Simon, behold Satan asked to have you, that he might sift you as wheat: but I made supplication for thee, that thy faith fail not: but do thou, when once thou hast turned again, stablish thy brethren." This certainly implies a special solicitude on the part of our Lord for St. Peter, that after the testing of his temptation and fall he may experience a real conversion and henceforth be able to establish and strengthen the other apostles. *The Acts of the Apostles* show how he began at once this work of guidance and leadership in the Church (Acts 1: 15 ff., 2: xiv ff., 3: xii ff., 4: 8 ff.) Professor Turner says of this passage from St. Luke's Gospel: "St. Luke's Gospel thus comes into line with St. Matthew and St. John in assigning to our Lord a solemn commiss˙ ⸱f leadership—we might almost say of a⸱ ⸱ority—to his chief apostle." (p. 74.)

With regard to the charge to St. Peter recorded in St. John's Gospel, "Feed my lambs . . . rule my sheep . . . feed my little sheep," the great French Modernist scholar, M. Loisy, has the following to say in his book, *"Le Quatrième Evangile"* (pp. 939–42):

The apostle is charged with the direction of the Christian flock in the place of Jesus. . . . In making Simon his Vicar, Jesus not only rehabilitates the renegade, but he confirms in his primacy the Prince of the Apostles. Perhaps we should say that he invests him with that office. Both in content and in form, as also in the characteristic use of the name *Simon,* this passage is parallel to the "Thou art Peter," of Matthew, and to the "Strengthen thy brethren," of Luke. These are three echoes of the same tradition, equally faithful to it as to their substance, although they may be more or less dependent, the one on the other, as to their origin. . . . It is very probable that a different term has been chosen for the third answer so as to imply a gradation: lambs, little sheep, sheep in general. These terms are not allegorical, in the sense that they represent three categories of members in the Christian society; taken singly or collectively, they designate the Christian flock as a whole; but the variety of the terms serves to show that there is to be no exception, and that all the faithful of Christ, whatever be their place in the community, are confided to the care of Simon Peter.

III

I should say, then, that from the start there is abundant evidence that the development of the Church was controlled by the fact that St. Peter was commissioned by our Lord to be the head of the Church on earth. But it is claimed by Anglicans that St. Peter faded out of the picture after the first chapters of the *Acts*, that St. Paul takes the center of the stage, and that to him is committed the care of all the Churches. Moreover, it is asserted that the early writers speak of the Roman See as founded by SS. Peter and Paul, not exclusively by St. Peter. "The evidence is positive," according to Dr. Barry, "that the Church organization developed in a quite different way from what it would have had the Petrine claims been recognized."

As to these Anglican assertions, let us see what Professor Cuthbert Turner has to say in the second of the articles to which I have already referred. He makes it clear that St. Paul's epistles are written to deal with special sets of circumstances in the Churches he had founded, and that we are not to look upon them as containing exhaustive descriptions of the faith and organization of the early Church. For example, they have a good deal to say about the Judaizing tendency in the Galatian churches. As against that tendency St. Paul contended that it was not necessary for the Gentile converts to submit to all the requirements of the Mosaic Law. The Gentile churches had been committed to his care, just as the Jewish churches were under the special supervision of St. Peter. "He that energized in Peter to an apostleship of the circumcision, energized in the same way in me for the Gentiles." (Gal. ii: 8.) Thus St. Peter and St. Paul were the special representatives of the Jewish Christians and the Gentile Christians. But the Jews came first: "To the Jew first, but also to the Gentile." This necessarily meant that St. Peter's position was superior to that of St. Paul. Indeed, St. Paul could not make a final ruling on the matter until he had gone to Jerusalem to consult St. Peter. In Galatians i: 18, St. Paul expressly says, "After three years, I went up to Jerusalem to see Peter, and abode with him fifteen days." Professor Turner says that to "see Peter" is not an adequate translation of the Greek ἱστορῆσαι Κηφᾶν. It means that he visited Cephas for the purpose of inquiry. The Greek word connotes "to admire and to learn." It is Professor Turner's belief that in all of St. Paul's epistles Peter loomed larger than the other apostles.

The first importance of the Church of Rome lay in the fact that it was a synthesis of the Jewish and Gentile elements of the Church. This is clearly brought out by the constant designation of SS. Peter and Paul as the founders of the Roman Church. They were the two witnesses, or martyrs, spoken of in Revelation xi: 8 as the principal victims of the Beast. This, according to Professor Turner, is the first expression in extant Christian literature of the combined commemoration of the two great apostles.

The early Church in Rome was naturally made up of both Jewish and Gentile converts. Therefore it was meet that they should be instructed and built up in the faith by both the apostle to the circumcision and the apostle to the uncircumcision. Thus the two conflicting strains of primitive Christianity were reconciled in the Roman Church. The fact that through the succeeding centuries that Church has always commemorated SS. Peter and Paul together is a strong guarantee that her presentation of the faith has included the best elements in the Jewish and Gentile contributions to Christianity. Sprinkled by the blood of these two great apostles the Roman Church soon became a hardy plant which resisted all the noxious growths of heresy.

Now let us take up the question of St. Peter's connection with the Church in Rome. The first epistle of St. Peter is commonly accepted as genuine. The next to the last verse of that epistle contains these words: "The church that is at Babylon, elected together with you, saluteth you; and so doth Mark, my son." Babylon, of course, refers to Rome, and this proves that St. Peter wrote this epistle from Rome. It might almost be called the first Papal Encyclical. We do not know just when the Church in Rome was founded. In a sense, St. Peter might be said to have founded the Roman Church, on the day of Pentecost, by converting the "strangers of Rome," who were present in Jerusalem at that time, and heard his great sermon. We know that after St. Peter left Jerusalem he appeared in Antioch (Gal. ii: 11). We know from the Roman historian Suetonius that there were Christians in Rome in the year 49. When St. Paul wrote his Epistle to the Romans in 54 or 55, he stated that their faith

was spoken of in the whole world (Romans i: 8).
We may assume that St. Paul delayed his visit to
Rome owing to the fact that Peter had preached
there. He explicitly states as his reason "Lest I should
build on another man's foundation." (Rom.
xv: 20.) He does not go in order to found a church
there, but merely to pay a visit on his way to Spain.
He addresses the Roman Christians with some def-
erence, and he honors them by his greatest theological treatise, "The public exposition of his gospel." [1]

If, then, St. Peter preceded St. Paul in Rome, it
is probable that his visit took place between his disappearance from Palestine in the year 44 and his
return to Jerusalem in 48—the "other place" of
Acts xii: 17 being Rome. St. Jerome, in his life of
St. Peter, written at the end of the fourth century,
states that Peter came to Rome "in the second year
of Claudius" or 42 A. D. There is therefore nothing
improbable in the tradition and the belief of all
early Catholic writers that St. Peter labored for
these few years in Rome. His martyrdom there at
a later period is vouched for by a fairly continuous
line of references in the documents from the time
of St. Clement on. There was, of course, a tradition
that he was there until the time of his martyrdom,
but it is reasonable to suppose that he must have

[1] R. B. Rackham, *The Acts of the Apostles*, p. 362.

felt some obligation as the apostle to the circumcision to make visits to the churches in Palestine.[1]

At any rate, we know that St. Peter returned to Jerusalem in A. D. 48 to be present at the Council of Jerusalem. This council has been the subject of much controversy. It certainly looks as if St. Peter's pronouncement controlled the decision of the council, very much in the same way as Pope Leo the Great's pronouncement, in his famous *Tome,* controlled the decision of the Council of Chalcedon. It was because of the revelation that St. Peter had received in connection with Cornelius, that he laid down the principle that the Gentile converts were not under obligation to follow all the requirements of the Mosaic Law. This became the decision of the council, as voiced by St. James, the Bishop of Jerusalem. The well-known Anglican scholar, Dr. F. J. Hort, in his book, *The Christian Ecclesia,* pp. 79–80, thus expresses his opinion of the council:

There is nothing in St. Luke's words which bears out what is often said, that St. James presided over the conference at Jerusalem. If he had, it would be strange that his name should never be mentioned separately at the beginning. In the decision speeches at the end, the lead

[1] For these last two paragraphs I am indebted to the valuable book by Shotwell and Loomis, *The See of Peter,* published by the Columbia University Press.

is taken by St. Peter, the foremost of the Twelve. Then, again, the words which begin his (St. James') conclusion, *Wherefore my judgment is,* cannot reasonably be understood as an authoritative pronouncement by himself independently.

As to the disappearance of St. Peter from the latter chapters of the *Acts,* it is interesting to read the opinion of such impartial scholars as Shotwell and Loomis (p. 49) that the "eloquent silence" of the second part of *Acts* with reference to Peter, loses some of the force of its argument against the Petrine claims when we recall the Pauline and partial character of its survey of the situation. "Because Peter drops out of sight in the *Acts,* it is not necessary to suppose that he dropped out of sight in the work of the Church. The first step in historical criticism is to recognize the inadequacy of one's sources. This is commented upon already in the *Muratorian Fragment* of about 180 A. D. Luke records only those things done in his own presence, 'As he plainly shows by leaving out the passion of Peter, and also the departure of Paul from town on his journey to Spain.'"

Chapter X

THE PETRINE TRADITION IN ROME

I

ONE of the most disturbing impressions I have ever received was when, in June of the year 1926, I stood for the first time before the great Basilica of St. Peter's in Rome and read the inscription at the base of the dome: *Tu es Petrus; et super hanc petram aedificabo ecclesiam meam.* At that moment something happened in my inner consciousness which shook the foundations of my life. The experience was repeated when, a little later, I knelt before the tomb of St. Peter. My faith in the Anglican Church then received a blow from which it has never recovered.

It is hard to see how anyone, after a careful study of the Gospels, can doubt that our Lord gave to St. Peter a primacy among the apostles, and a jurisdiction over the whole Church. It is equally difficult for anyone with a knowledge of history to doubt that the Bishops of Rome since the beginning

have professed to be the heirs of St. Peter's powers
and prerogatives in the apostolic college. The important question with which I must now deal is
whether there is a historical link connecting St.
Peter with the Roman bishopric. Were the powers
conferred by Christ upon St. Peter merely personal
powers which were to be exercised only during his
lifetime? If so, they have no significance for the
Church today. To quote the words of Shotwell and
Loomis (*The See of Peter*, p. 65): "A grant of
rights conferred by however competent an authority, upon an individual almost two thousand years
ago, can have no vital import for anyone today, unless the individual has left a line of successors who
have inherited and continuously exercised those
rights down to the present time." On the other
hand, the Roman Church would in any case have
exercised a powerful influence on Christianity, because of its location in the Imperial City, the size
and character of its membership, and the fact that
it had profited by St. Paul's teaching and martyrdom. But its Bishop would have had legally no
greater powers than the Bishops of Antioch and
Alexandria, which also could boast of apostolic
founders.

This historical link is supplied by the Petrine
tradition, which connects St. Peter so closely with

the Roman bishopric, that he, either with or without St. Paul "may be considered to have been its originator, and to have bequeathed to it as its particular legacy the authority which his Master had once entrusted to him." (Shotwell and Loomis, p. 64.) We need not be surprised if it is a meager tradition. "One characteristic of primitive Christian literature is that it explains and defines so little, that it confidently looks for a speedy end of the world, heeds only the immediate emergency, and addresses itself to persons who understand the situation as the author does, and for whom a hint will suffice." (p. 63.)

One of the baffling mysteries of early Christian history is the complete disappearance of all the apostles except SS. Peter and Paul. "Save for a few episodes of St. John's old age, preserved by Polycarp and repeated by Eusebius, nothing but dubious and hesitating tradition remains about the later years of any apostle but Peter and Paul." (Shotwell and Loomis, p. 63, footnote.) During the first three centuries the names Peter and Paul were the only names taken from the Bible that were borne by Gentile Christians. It is absurd to say that "Peter faded from the picture"; the fact is that everyone else but Peter and Paul faded from the picture. Harnack goes so far as to say: "Probably, then, it is not too hazardous to affirm that the Church really had never more than two apostles in the true sense of the term . . . viz., Paul and Peter—unless perhaps we add John of Ephesus." (*The Mission and Expansion of Christianity*, Moffatt's translation, Vol. I, p. 351.)

II

One of the first and most striking expressions of the claim of the Bishop of Rome to jurisdiction over the whole Church is to be found in St. Clement's first letter to the Church in Corinth, written in A. D. 96. This is scarcely a generation after St. Peter was martyred in Rome. St. Clement stands second after Linus in the early list of Roman Bishops, which names Linus as the successor of the apostles. He is probably the same Clement whom St. Paul mentions in his letter from Rome to the Philippians. The Christians at Corinth had rebelled against their hierarchy, and had driven out their presbyters. The Bishop of Rome writes to them, not merely as one neighbor to another, to express his regret for what they have done. He commands them, with an arbitrary tone of authority, which could hardly be exceeded by any medieval Pope, to submit themselves again in obedience to their ecclesiastical superiors.

Our apostles also knew through our Lord Jesus Christ that there would be strife over the title of bishop. For this reason, therefore, inasmuch as they had received perfect foreknowledge, they appointed to office those whom we have mentioned and afterwards made provision that when they should fall asleep, other approved men should succeed to their ministry. We, accordingly, believe that it is not right to dismiss from their ministry those who were appointed by them or afterwards by other eminent men with the consent of the whole Church, and who have served the flock of Christ without fault, humbly, peaceably, and disinterestedly, and received for a long time the good testimony of everyone. For our sin will not be small if we remove from the episcopate those who have blamelessly and holily offered its sacrifices. . . . You, therefore, that laid the foundation of sedition, submit yourselves unto the presbyters and receive correction unto repentance, bending the knees of your hearts. Learn to be submissive and lay aside the proud and boastful stubbornness of your tongues. . . . But if some be disobedient unto the words spoken by him (God) through us, let them see that they will involve themselves in grave transgression and danger, but we shall be guiltless of their sin. . . . For you will give us joy and gladness if you are obedient to the things which we have written through the Holy Spirit, and root out the wicked passions of your jealousy in compliance with the request we have made in this letter for peace and harmony. And we have sent you faithful and prudent men that have walked among us

blamelessly from youth to old age, and they shall be
witnesses between you and us.[1]

Surely it is extraordinary that the Bishop of Rome
should send categorical orders to a church in Greece.
The apostle John was still living at Ephesus, and
would have been the natural one to interfere in the
affairs of the Corinthian Church. Why was St.
Clement the one to restore order? Obviously, because the Bishop of Rome, as successor of St. Peter,
had jurisdiction over the whole Church.

In the early days of the Church the Roman
Bishop spoke as the guardian of an authoritative
tradition, and his position as guardian was second
to none. Even when the Eastern Churches insisted
that their traditions were older, and perhaps even
more sacred, this Western Bishop spoke on, regardless of protest or denunciation. According to Shotwell and Loomis, (p. 221) the first authentic incident related of a Roman Bishop has to do with a
visit paid by the aged Polycarp, Bishop of Smyrna,
to Anicetus, Bishop of Rome. St. Polycarp was at
this time ninety years old, and yet he took this long
journey to Rome to take up with the Roman Bishop
the method of fixing the date of Easter. He in-

[1] Shotwell and Loomis, pp. 237-39.

formed Anicetus that the Roman mode of fixing
the date was not that which he himself had learned
from the practice of the apostle, St. John. This,
however, does not affect the decision of Anicetus.
He honors Polycarp by yielding to him the administration of the Eucharist in the Church of St. John
Lateran, but he insists on retaining the method of
reckoning Easter which had always prevailed in the
Roman Church. This method later became universal.

St. Ignatius, Bishop of Antioch, on his journey to
Rome to be martyred (116 A. D.), wrote letters to
all the leading Churches, including Rome. These
letters show that by that time the diocesan bishop
was everywhere regarded as the embodiment of divine authority and grace. Without him, no sacrament was valid. Apart from him there could be no
Church. He says, "Let that Eucharist be regarded as
valid which is celebrated by the bishop, or by one
whom he appoints. Wheresoever the bishop appears,
there let the people be, even as where Jesus Christ
is, there is the Catholic Church." [1] To this Eastern
bishop the Roman Church appears "to stand upon
a level somewhat above that of the others to which
he writes. To no other does he address quite such
ardent phrases of praise for its unwavering stead-

[1] Shotwell and Loomis, p. 240.

fastness and faith." [1] Incidentally, his letter to the Romans contains early evidence that SS. Peter and Paul administered the Roman Church. He says, "I do not command you, as Peter and Paul did. They were apostles; I am a convict." Thus he assumes it to be well known to his hearers that SS. Peter and Paul had preached in person to the faithful at Rome. St. Ignatius begs that they will not use their great influence with the Imperial authorities to prevent his martyrdom. This shows that at this time the Roman Church included many influential persons. The passage in the letter to the Romans which bears especially on the subject of the jurisdiction of the Bishop of Rome is as follows: "To the Church that is beloved and enlightened through the will of Him who hath willed all things that are, according to the love of Jesus Christ, our God, even to her that presides in the land of the Romans, worthy of God, worthy of honor, worthy of blessing, worthy of praise, worthy of prosperity, worthy in her purity, and foremost in love." These last words, "foremost in love," cannot be thus translated, because the word for love is genitive and not dative in the Greek. The word translated love, is used by Ignatius for the Church several times. Therefore this phrase is best translated, according to Funk and

[1] Shotwell and Loomis, p. 239.

Harnack, "president of the bond of love," meaning
of the whole body of Christians. This is what Harnack has to say of St. Ignatius in his *History of
Dogma,* Vol. IV, p. 486:

> However much one may tone down all excessive ex-
> pressions in his letter to the Romans, this much is clear,
> that Ignatius has admitted in fact a precedence of the
> Roman community in the circle of her sisters, and that
> he knows of an energetic and perpetual activity on the
> part of this community in supporting and teaching
> others. . . . Even the elaborate address shows that he
> honors and greets this community as the most distin-
> guished in Christendom.

III

I wish I had space to speak of Hegesippus of
Syria (160–175) who tells how, as a security for
the genuineness of the Roman tradition, he com-
piled a list of the Roman Bishops through whom the
true faith had been transmitted during the hundred
years from the apostles Peter and Paul to Anicetus;
of Soter (166–174), who succeeded Anicetus as
Bishop of Rome, and wrote a pastoral letter to the
Corinthians which they treasured equally with that
of St. Clement; and of Bishop Eleutherus (175–
188), who succeeded Soter as Bishop of Rome, and
condemned the heresy of the Gnostic Marcion, a

wealthy and influential member of the Roman congregation, as well as the new Puritan Montanist
heresy that had sprung up in Phrygia. (Shotwell
and Loomis, pp. 248–261.)

But I must pass on to the testimony of St.
Irenaeus (130–200), the Bishop of Lyons in Gaul.
Irenaeus was a Greek who had lived in Smyrna and
had been taught by St. Polycarp, who remembered
the apostle, St. John. In the year 177, while he was
still a priest, a report of the Montanist disturbances
in Asia had reached the Church at Lyons, and
Irenaeus was despatched to Rome to seek guidance
and counsel from the Bishop Eleutherus. He used
the opportunity to gather the material for his book,
Against Heresies, especially the Gnostic schools of
Valentinus and Marcion. In combating these heresies he drew upon the Church's two authentic
sources of knowledge: the four Gospels and the
tradition bequeathed by the apostles to their successors. He says, every apostolic Church has its own
legacy of tradition handed on as a sacred charge to
the bishop, but he will let one Church suffice as
an example, namely, "the very great and ancient
and illustrious Church founded and organized at
Rome by the two glorious apostles, Peter and Paul,
and the faith declared to mankind and handed
down to our own time through its bishops in their

succession." (Shotwell and Loomis, p. 267.) This is
followed by a very important passage which has
been much discussed. Unfortunately we have it only
in the Latin translation, as the Greek of Irenaeus'
original work has been lost. Catholic and Protestant
scholars translate this passage differently, but as the
great German scholar, Professor Harnack, translates
it in the same way as do the Catholic scholars
(Harnack's History of Dogma, Vol. II, p. 157,
note 3) I have adopted this translation: "With this
Church (in Rome) on account of its preëminent
authority, every Church must be in agreement, that
is, the faithful everywhere, among whom the tradition of the apostles has been continuously preserved." This affords striking testimony to the universal jurisdiction of the Roman See at the end of
the second century. Every Church founded by the
apostles had sovereign authority, but that of Rome
was preëminent; and believers in all parts of the
world must agree with this Church if they were to
be faithful to the apostolic tradition.

Victor was Bishop of Rome from 188–198. In
him we see the same claim to universal jurisdiction
over the whole Church that had been made by his
predecessors, but expressed with greater vigor and
authority. According to Shotwell and Loomis, "His
pontificate marks the passing of the primitive, un-

ostentatious stage in the history of the Roman See, and the opening of a new and infinitely more ambitious era." [1] He detected the Adoptionist heresy lurking in the teaching of Theodotus of Byzantium, who taught that Christ was a man like other men, though qualified peculiarly by divine grace to perform his lofty mission to the world. Victor excommunicated him, as Eleutherus had expelled Marcion from the Church. Theodotus proceeded to found an independent sect.

The most striking act of Victor was the excommunication of the whole province of Asia Minor because the bishops of that province persisted in celebrating Easter, according to the Jewish reckoning, on the fourteenth day of the month Nisan, whether it came on a Sunday or not. Irenaeus of Lyons, who himself followed the Roman use in the celebration of Easter, remonstrated with Victor on the ground that he ought not to cut off whole Churches of God for holding to an ancient custom. True to his name, he was trying to act as peacemaker; but the significant fact is, that he did not question Victor's authority. He merely questioned the wisdom of its being exercised on a mere matter of discipline, with such catastrophic effects. As a matter of fact, the successors of Victor allowed the

[1] Shotwell and Loomis, p. 274.

contention to drop, although the Roman use was soon adopted by the universal Church.

We next come to Tertullian, the African lawyer, who lived in Carthage from 160–235. His book against the heresies of his day (*De Praescriptione Haereticorum*) throws much light on the position of the Roman Church in his time. To him the argument against heresy drawn from Catholic tradition was even more decisive than the argument from Scripture, for the heretics could interpret Scripture in their own way. There could be no dispute about the meaning of tradition, inasmuch as the transmitter of tradition, who was always the bishop of an apostolic see, possessed *ipso facto* the right to interpret it. According to Tertullian, the chief depositaries of trustworthy tradition were the apostolic Churches, and he dwelt eloquently upon the wealth of such tradition concentrated at Rome. He challenged the heretics to prove that any of their Churches were of apostolic foundation. He says, "Let them produce the original records of their Churches, let them unfold the roll of their bishops, running down in due succession from the beginning, so that their bishop may show as his ordainer and predecessor, one of the apostles, or one of the apostles' disciples!" I will quote the passage which contains the panegyric of the Roman Church:

Come, then, you who would better exercise your wits about the business of your own salvation, recall the various apostolic churches in which the actual chairs of the apostles are still standing in their places, in which their own authentic letters are read, repeating the voice and calling up the face of each of them severally. Achaia is very near you, where you have Corinth. If you are not far from Macedonia, you have Philippi. If you can travel into Asia, you have Ephesus. But if you are near Italy, you have Rome, whence also our authority is derived close at hand. How happy is that church on which the apostles poured forth all their teaching, together with their blood! Where Peter endured a passion like his Lord's! Where Paul won his crown in a death like John's! Where the apostle John was first plunged unhurt into boiling oil and then banished to an island! See what she has learned, what she has taught, what fellowship she has had with our churches too in Africa! One God does she acknowledge, the Creator of the universe, and Christ Jesus born of the Virgin Mary, Son of God the Creator and the resurrection of the flesh. To the writings of the evangelists and the apostles she adds the law and the prophets and therefrom she imbibes her faith. This faith she seals with water, arrays with the Holy Ghost, feeds with the Eucharist, strengthens with martyrdom and against this faith and practice she admits no gainsayer.

Later on, when he became a Montanist, Tertullian fell under the censure of the Church and he changed his tone about the authority of the apostolic see. Thereafter he found it convenient to teach that the power of the keys was conferred upon Peter personally, and that the same power belongs to all spiritual men, whether apostles or prophets (Shotwell and Loomis, p. 303). This somewhat resembles the modern Protestant doctrine of the priesthood of all believers. Nevertheless, Tertullian's attack on the Petrine claims of the Roman Bishop supply further evidence that those claims were widely accepted at the beginning of the third century.

IV

have always been told that St. Cyprian, the Bishop of Carthage, who was born about the year 200 and martyred in 258, was one of the most vigorous opponents of the Petrine claims of the Bishop of Rome. It behooves us therefore to look into his history and ascertain what was his real position. He was bishop during the Decian persecution, and his correspondence with the Church in Rome during that period throws much light on the situation both in Rome and Carthage, especially in regard to the treatment of those who had apostatized under persecution. He took a middle ground between the Puritans who held that there should be no forgiveness for the sin of apostasy, and the easy-going, worldly group, who believed that all the lapsed should be taken back without repentance. Cyprian maintained that each case should be dealt with on its merits, but that all should be placed under penitential discipline, and after they had demonstrated that they were penitent, they were to be received back into the communion of the Church.

In his brilliant treatise, *On the Unity of the Catholic Church,* St. Cyprian lays stress on the authority of the bishops as successors of the apostles, and the necessity of submitting to their authority, if one is to remain in the Church. All bishops share equally in the right to bind and loose, yet the power of the keys was bestowed on Peter alone, and he alone was made the foundation of the Church. One man was chosen for honor at the outset, in order that through him might be symbolized the unity of the episcopate and the Church. Peter, and after him his successors at Rome, stand as corporeal reminders of the unity of the Catholic Church. But neither Peter nor the Roman Bishops have any higher powers than the other Apostles and bishops. Following is the passage which sets forth Cyprian's views:

Upon one man the Lord builds the Church, and although He grants to all the Apostles after his resurrection an equal power, . . . yet, that He might make clear their unity, He established by his authority that unity at the beginning, as if it originated in one man. Assuredly, the rest of the Apostles were equal to Peter, endowed with the same partnership in honor and power, but the beginning was made in unity, that the Church of Christ might be manifested to be one.

In one of Cyprian's epistles, warning against dealings of any kind with Felicissimus and five other priests who had communicated with the lapsed, Cyprian says: "They who themselves have deserted the Church are preventing the Church from bringing back and recalling the lapsed. There is one God and one Christ and one Church, and one *cathedra*, established upon Peter by the word of the Lord. Another altar cannot be erected nor a new priesthood created, beside the one altar and the one priesthood."

The Anglican Church has no greater authority on early Christian literature than Professor Cuthbert H. Turner of Oxford. It is interesting therefore to read his interpretation of the position of St. Cyprian, which he has given us in his article on SS. Peter and Paul, in *Theology* for October, 1926.

Cyprian has a clear-cut theory, of which the first element is the essential identity of the episcopal and apostolic office, and the second is the essential identity of the position of Peter and of his successors at Rome. What Peter was among the Apostles, that his successor was, among Catholic bishops, the symbol and source of unity. What Peter had not among the Apostles—that is, any difference in dignity or authority—that the Pope had not in regard to other members of the episcopate. In each case there was, so to say, a college and a head. But the head could not act apart from his colleagues; moreover, though the Bishop of Rome was successor of St. Peter, and inherited all the prerogative that Peter had in relation to the other Apostles, there was of course one thing that he could not inherit. Peter was the original foundation on which Christ built his Church. Cyprian would never have said that Church was founded on Peter and his successors.

After the martyrdom of Fabian, Bishop of Rome, the Roman Church for a time put off the election of a new Bishop. They preferred to wait until the severity of the Decian persecution had passed. It is an interesting fact that during the vacancy in the Roman episcopate the clergy of Rome continued to exercise a supervision over the affairs of the African Church. Their letters to Cyprian contained many wise suggestions which enabled him to deal firmly with the problem of the lapsed. This proves that at this early date the Church in the city of Rome regarded itself as entrusted with an authority of governance over the whole Church. This authority did not depend simply upon the position of the Bishop of Rome as the successor of St. Peter, but also upon the fact that the glorious Apostles Peter and Paul had been the founders of the Roman tradition.

Chapter XI

THE REGULATIVE AUTHORITY OF THE BISHOPS OF ROME

I

IN my study of the historical development of the Papacy in the first three centuries, I have made what is for me a startling discovery. I have found that all the fundamental laws and institutions of Catholicism were first formulated and perfected in the Church of the city of Rome, and later imposed upon the other dioceses and provinces of the Church throughout the Empire. I am primarily indebted for this discovery to the monumental work on the *History of Dogma* by the eminent German Protestant historian, Professor Harnack. Especially in his *Excursus, Catholic and Roman,* in the second volume, he makes it abundantly clear that we owe to the Church in the city of Rome the Apostles' Creed, the New Testament Canon and the traditional form of the apostolic ministry.

As early as the year 180 the Roman Church possessed a clearly formulated baptismal confession of faith known as the Roman Creed, and she declared this to be the apostolic rule by which all Christian teaching was to be measured. That creed was substantially the same as the Apostles' Creed which we recite today. It was because of this creed that the Roman Church in the first three centuries was enabled to distinguish true doctrine from false with special exactness. That is why men like Irenaeus, Tertullian, Cyprian and Origen constantly appealed to her to decide on matters of doctrine and practice. In no other Church do we find this apostolic rule of faith formulated so early; but later on it became universally accepted.

The New Testament Canon as we have it today is likewise first traceable to the Church of Rome. In other Churches other books were read as New Testament Scriptures, such as the Gospel of Peter, the Gospel of the Egyptians, or Tatian's *Diatessaron*. The Canon was definitely fixed at Rome toward the close of the second century. Alexandria did not reach the same stage until forty years later. Moreover, textual investigations have shown that the Western readings—that is to say, the Roman text of the New Testament—were, after the third century, adopted in the Oriental manuscripts of the Bible. Thus the Eastern Churches received their

New Testament from Rome and used it to correct their copies of the books read in public worship.

The developed form of the apostolic ministry was first settled at Rome, and later became universal. At the beginning there were undoubtedly differences in different sections of the Church. In some places presbyters were almost on a par with bishops; in other places all the presbyters were bishops; in other places certain bishops were superior to other bishops. Rome is the first place which we can prove to have constructed a list of bishops reaching back to the apostles, as we learn from St. Irenaeus. The apostolic succession of bishops was first made a principle of Church government in Rome, and formed the basis for all later claims of sovereignty for the episcopate. Not only do we owe the threefold ministry of bishops, priests and deacons, which prevails today both in the West and in the East to the Roman Church; but the lower orders of deacons, acolytes, readers, gate-keepers and exorcists are first found in Rome. This distinction of higher and lower clergy gradually spread from Rome to the rest of Christendom. This momentous fact, that the mold of the Christian ministry first became hardened and fixed at Rome, seems to me to furnish the only basis on which the assertions of Professor

Streeter can be met by Catholics. In his recent book, entitled *The Primitive Church,* he says:

Perhaps the greatest obstacle (to reunion) is the belief, entertained more or less explicitly by most bodies of Christians, that there is some one form of Church order, which alone is primitive; and which therefore alone possesses the sanction of apostolic precedent. Our review of the historical evidence has shown this belief to be an illusion. In the primitive Church no one system of Church order prevailed. Everywhere there was readiness to experiment, and where circumstance seemed to demand it, to change.

It is extremely difficult to disprove this statement of Professor Streeter's from the standpoint of Anglo-Catholicism. It looks very much as if there were conflicting varieties of ministerial authority in the primitive Church of the first century. The fact that cannot be denied is that the system of Church order first became fixed in the Roman Church, and the authority of Rome imposed its acceptance in all parts of the Catholic Church. In this way only can we contradict Professor Streeter and insist that in the primitive Church one system of Church order did in fact prevail.

What happened in regard to the ministry happened in all other matters, as can be proved from the Alexandrian Church alone. As Harnack says

(Vol. II, p. 150, note 2), "Up to the end of the second century the Alexandrian Church had none of the Catholic and apostolic standards and none of the corresponding institutions as found in the Roman Church; her writer, Clement, was also 'as little acquainted with the West as was Homer.' In the course of the first half of the third century she received those standards and institutions."

How are we to account for this supreme regulative authority of the Roman Church? Harnack attributes it to the fact that she did thus impose her standards and institutions on the rest of the Church, together with the fact that as early as 180 this Church could point to a series of bishops reaching in uninterrupted succession from the glorious Apostles Peter and Paul. He says (Vol. II, p. 159): "All these causes combined to convert the Christian communities into a real confederation under the primacy of the Roman Church (and subsequently under the leadership of her bishops)." But surely Harnack is arguing in a circle. We cannot explain the authority of the Roman Church by the fact that she exercised that authority. It is more logical to account for it by some inherent right or power which led the rest of the Church to accept her leadership. I know it is the custom of Anglicans to attribute the authority of the Roman Church to the central importance of the city of Rome in the Empire. Undoubtedly that contributed greatly to her prestige, but it comes far short of accounting for all the facts. Otherwise, the Patriarch of Constantinople would have become the ruling bishop in the Church when the seat of the Empire was transferred to that city from Rome.

Three facts must be kept in mind in conjunction with one another if we are to understand the special prerogative of the Roman Church: the fact that Rome was the capital of the Empire; the fact that St. Peter was given by our Lord jurisdiction over the whole Christian flock; and the fact that the Church in Rome was founded by the combined labors of SS. Peter and Paul, the Apostle to the Jews and the Apostle to the Gentiles, and that both were martyred and buried there. Any one of these facts alone would have been insufficient to account for the subsequent authority of the Roman Church. May we not believe that St. Peter was divinely guided to go to Rome because it was the capital of the world? Jesus Christ, Peter, and Rome—taken together—explain the authority of the Roman Church.

II

According to Dr. Barry's letter, the Anglican theory is that the organization of the Church was not developed under the direction of Rome, nor was the Church's conception of authority Roman; its development was conciliar, its appeals were to the voice of the episcopate.

This is of course the theory which I have heretofore held, but there have been difficulties in holding this theory which I have never been able to surmount. The chief difficulty is that in some sections the authority of the Church is muffled; she never speaks with a clear and certain voice. The bishops of the Anglican Church do not all teach the same faith; the teachings of some of them, if not formally heretical, are at least ambiguous and open to heretical interpretation. Many of the Eastern Orthodox bishops, even the occupants of the great patriarchal sees, have been Monophysite or Nestorian in their Christology. Neither Anglicans nor Orthodox can be sure that in following the guidance of their bishops they are true to the Catholic faith. We cannot always be appealing to a general council to clear up our uncertainties.

There is, however, one group of bishops scattered throughout the whole world who always teach the same faith, the bishops who are in communion with the See of Peter. It is perfectly evident why this unity of doctrine has continuously been maintained by the Roman episcopate. The reason is that its mem-

bers are all united with the center and source of
unity, namely, the Bishop of Rome. He is the key-
stone of the arch. Without the supreme authority
of the Papacy, Roman Catholic bishops would soon
fall into disagreement and conflict, as have the other
bishops who have rejected that authority. This is a
marvelous testimony to the supernatural character
of the Roman Catholic Church, that she proves to
all the world that our Lord's prayer has been answered: "That they may be one, even as we are one;
I in them and thou in me, that they may be made
perfect in one; and that the world may know that
thou hast sent me, and hast loved them as thou
hast loved me." (St. John xvii: 22–23.)

What, then, are we to say of the seven ecumenical
councils? Did they supplant the authority of the
Bishop of Rome? Did they defy him and set him at
naught? Or did they act under his guidance and in
submission to his authority? Did they in any way define or limit his jurisdiction over the whole Church?
These are important questions, and to them I must
now address myself. In my study of the Councils I
have found much valuable help in a recent book by
an Anglican clergyman, the Reverend S. Herbert
Scott, entitled *The Eastern Churches and the Papacy*.
(London, Sheed and Ward, 1928.) The book is a dis-
sertation approved for a research doctorate degree

in the University of Oxford. This book has been for me an eye-opener. Heretofore I have always studied the Eastern Church from an Oriental standpoint, and with reference to the ecumenical councils. It is much more illuminating to study it from the Western standpoint, with a special view to its relations with the Bishop of Rome.

The General Councils were not the normal means through which the Church declared her mind. They met only at great intervals, and then only because a crisis had arisen. As Duchesne points out in his *Early History of the Church* (English translation, Vol. I, p. 389), "it was not until the reign of Constantine that the Church introduced the ecumenical council, an institution which, it must be acknowledged, was never very workable, and never succeeded in taking a place among the regular organs of Church life." The seven ecumenical councils were all held in the East, and dealt largely with Eastern heresies. They were usually, if not always, convened by the Emperor. They were almost like provincial synods of the East, for very few Western bishops were present at them. It is extraordinary, therefore, that the Bishop of Rome should have had anything to do with them, or they with him. Yet we find that he was represented by his legates at all of them. The pronouncements of these legates carried great weight, and often put an end to all controversy. The decrees of the council were of no force unless confirmed by the Bishop of Rome. Indeed, it looks very much as if what made a general council ecumenical was the fact that its decrees were accepted by the apostolic see. Duchesne says, in his *Separated Churches*, p. 45, "Those councils belonged to us as much as to them; nay, more than to them. I know well that they were held in the East, that the Emperors residing or governing in the East procured their assembly. But for the most part they only represent an orthodox Roman victory over an Eastern heresy; or, to speak more charitably, a remedy applied by the Latin Church to her Greek sister, infected by some doctrinal malady." The following heretics, who were condemned by the ecumenical councils, were all Easterners: Arius, Eusebius of Nicomedia, Macedonius, Apollinaris, Eutyches, Patriarch of Constantinople, and Dioscorus, Patriarch of Alexandria.

I have been brought up on the theory that the decrees of the ecumenical councils are authoritative evidence as to what constitutes the Catholic faith. Now, the records and documents of these seven councils show that the Eastern Church all along believed and accepted:

(1) The primacy of the Bishop of Rome.

(2) That the Bishop of Rome had that primacy because he was the successor of St. Peter.

(3) That Christ had given headship of the Church to Peter; therefore it was "of divine right."

(4) That that headship was passed on and was inherited by his successors in the See of Rome. Therefore the Bishops of Rome held their headship *de jure divino* (by divine right).

(5) The documents of the Councils of Ephesus and Chalcedon (to mention no others) show that these Eastern councils, by promulgating the sentence of Pope Celestine on Nestorius, and the exposition of the Catholic faith set forth in the *Tome* of Pope Leo the Great, acknowledged the power and right of the Roman Bishop to declare authoritatively to the universal Church what was the Catholic faith.[1]

In none of the seven ecumenical councils is there any evidence that the claims of the Bishop of Rome to supreme jurisdiction by right of his succession from Peter, Prince of the Apostles, were denied. The Popes make claims which are voiced publicly in the general councils and meet with acceptance. In the Council of Chalcedon, after the *Tome* of Pope Leo had been read, all the bishops shouted in acclamation, "It is the faith of the apostles, it is the

[1] Scott, *The Eastern Churches and the Papacy*, p. 352.

faith of the Fathers. Thus we all believe . . . Peter has spoken by the mouth of Leo."

I have already spoken, in a previous chapter, of the 28th canon of the Council of Chalcedon. As those who oppose the Petrine claims of the Papacy have based many of their arguments on this celebrated canon, it is desirable that we should go into it a little further. The canon runs as follows:

The Fathers rightly attribute to old Rome privileges which correspond to its political importance. And it is by a similar sentiment that the five hundred Bishops have accorded to new Rome equal privileges, rightly judging that, having both the Emperor and his senate, it ought to enjoy the same advantages, to have the same importance in ecclesiastical order, and to keep in all things the second rank after old Rome.

It is argued by the critics of the Papacy that this canon proves that the Papal claims were based entirely on the political importance of the city of Rome. In considering this argument, we should bear in mind certain facts. In the first place, there are ancient manuscripts which bear the signatures of the legates from Rome after the first twenty-seven canons. In the second place, when the Archdeacon Aetius brought forth the question of the privileges of the Church of Constantinople, the Roman legates said that the question was not one which came within the terms of their commission. They therefore withdrew from the council, and most of the Fathers had already left for home. In the third place, only eighty-four signed this 28th canon, although there were six hundred and thirty members of the council. Finally, the canon is only concerned with the patriarchal position of Rome, not its primacy.[1]

It may equally well be argued that the existence of this canon tells rather in favor of the Roman claims than against them, for it begins as follows: "We define first of all that the primacy and the eminent honor following the canons being safeguarded for the most holy Archbishop of ancient Rome, it is also necessary that the most holy Archbishop of the Imperial City, new Rome, Constantinople, enjoy the same privileges of honor and receive authoritatively the power to ordain the metropolitans of Asia, of Pontus and of Thrace." The legates opposed this canon on the ground that it threatened the honor belonging by ancient conciliar enactment to Alexandria and Antioch, which had always ranked second and third after Rome. The canon does not deny the primacy of Rome; on the contrary, it formally recognizes it.

As I have said in a previous chapter, Pope Leo the Great refused to accept this canon, but he never for

[1] Scott, p. 193.

one moment saw in it an attack on his primacy. He
certainly would have seen it if it had been there, and
would have vigorously protested against it on that
ground. He rejected it because of its depriving
Alexandria and Antioch of the patriarchal rank that
had always belonged to them. One of the best criticisms of this 28th canon of Chalcedon which I have
seen is that of St. Methodius, the Byzantine Apostle of the Slavs. This was discovered in recent years
in a Slav manuscript of the twelfth century, and
published by an Orthodox Russian writer, A. Pav-
lov. It is quoted by Dr. Scott on p. 198, and reads
as follows:

It is necessary to know that this decision was not
accepted by the Blessed Pope Leo. . . . And it is not
true, as this canon affirms, that the holy Fathers have
accorded the primacy and honor to old Rome because it
was the capital of the Empire. But it is from on high
that it began, it is of grace divine that this primacy has
derived its origin. Peter, the most exalted of the apostles,
heard from the mouth of our Lord these words (S. Matt.
16: 17). This is why he possesses among the hierarchs
preëminent rank and the first see. It is notorious besides that although Emperors have dwelt at Milan and
Ravenna, and that their palaces are found there to our
own day, these cities have not received on that account
the primacy. For the dignity and the preëminence of the
priestly hierarchy have not been established by the

favor of the civil power, but by divine choice, and by apostolic authority. . . . How would it be possible because of an earthly Emperor to displace divine gifts and apostolic privileges and to introduce innovations into the prescriptions of the immaculate faith? Immovable indeed, unto the end, are the privileges of old Rome. So, in so far as being set over all the Churches, the Pontiff of Rome has no need to betake himself to all the holy ecumenical councils, but without his participation manifested by the sending of some of his subordinates, every ecumenical council is non-existent, and it is he who renders legal everything that has been decided in the council.

III

I have always found difficulty in the theory that a general council became an ecumenical council when its decisions were accepted by the whole Church. One difficulty of this theory is that the Church must wait a long time to find out whether a general council has settled anything. The acceptance of its decisions by the whole Church might take a hundred years or more. In the meantime the faithful must be left in the dark as to what they are to believe. Another difficulty is that none of the seven ecumenical councils have, as a matter of fact, been accepted by the whole Church. There have always been bishops and priests, as well as whole sections of the Church, that have refused to accept some of their decrees. This is notably true of the Anglican Communion. If the Anglican Church is to be considered a part of the Catholic Church, then the fact that the pronouncements of these seven councils are not commonly accepted by all Anglican bishops as authoritative in matters of faith, must invalidate their ecumenicity. What Anglican bishop would ever dream of condemning a priest in his diocese for holding Monophysite or Monothelite views on the Incarnation, because such views had been declared unorthodox at Chalcedon or Constantinople? Any such claim would have no weight in an ecclesiastical trial for heresy.

It seems necessary, therefore, to find some other test of ecumenicity for the general councils. If we make a study of the seven ecumenical councils we find that there are two features which they all had in common: They were all convened by the Emperor and they were all accepted by the Bishop of Rome. In the cases of some of the councils the call was issued jointly by the Emperor and the Pope. In some of the councils Papal legates presided, in others someone designated by the Emperor presided. There is apparently no uniformity on these points. Now, certainly no one would maintain that the fact that they were called together by the Emperor made them

ecumenical. That would mean the complete domination of the Church by the State. There is, however,
much to be said for the contention that these particular councils became ecumenical because their
acts were ratified and confirmed by the Bishop of
Rome. He was recognized as the supreme authority
in the Church, and his acceptance of the seven great
councils meant that they were accepted by the whole
Church, and that their canons possessed ecumenical
authority.

Whatever view we take as to how these seven general councils became ecumenical, their pronouncements on the nature of the authority possessed by
the Bishop of Rome are of the utmost importance.
I have space to mention only three of them. At the
Council of Ephesus (431) the Papal legate, Philip,
described St. Peter as "the Prince and Head of the
Apostles, the pillar of the faith and the foundation
of the Catholic Church," and declared that St. Peter
"up to this time, and always, lives in his successors
and gives judgment," and he refers to Pope Celestine
as "the successor and representative of St. Peter." The
Fathers of this council, in giving sentence against
Nestorius, prefaced their anathema with these
words: "Necessarily impelled by the canons and by
the letter of our most holy Father and fellow-minis-
ter, Celestine, Bishop of the Roman Church."

At the Council of Chalcedon (451) the Papal legate, Paschasinus, called the Pope "the head of all the Churches"; and the Fathers of the council, in their letter to the Emperor Marcian, spoke of the Pope as the "invulnerable champion," whom "God provided," and in their letter to Pope Leo described him as the "head," of which they were the "members," and as him to whom "was intrusted by the Saviour the guarding of the vine," the Church.

At the Council of Constantinople (680) the Fathers of the Council wrote to Pope Agatho: "We commit to thee as the chief ruler of the universal Church, standing on the firm rock of the faith, what is to be done, to give effect to the decisions of the Council"; and described the Pope's letter to the Emperor as "uttered about divine truths by the chief head of the apostles." [1]

A study of the ecumenical councils makes it clear that the struggle against heresy in the East drove the orthodox leaders of the Eastern Churches to take refuge at Rome or to look to Rome for help against their heretical Emperors, bishops, and other teachers. The Bishop of Rome was the one free and dependable religious power in the whole world. It may be that at times some of the Eastern bishops

[1] I am indebted for these quotations to the article on "Councils," in the *Encyclopedia of Religion and Ethics*, Vol. IV, p. 189, col. 2.

and patriarchs did not like to admit this fact, but the logic of events compelled them to do so. It is easy to make an impressive list of the great saints and Fathers of the East who acknowledged the Bishop of Rome as the successor of St. Peter and, by virtue of that succession, the supreme guardian of the orthodox faith. This is strikingly brought out in the work of Vladimir Soloviev on *Russia and the Universal Church*,[1] from which I have space to quote only the following:

As a member of the true and venerable Eastern Orthodox, or Greco-Russian Church, which speaks neither through an anti-canonical synod nor through the servants of the secular power, but through the voice of her great Fathers and Doctors, I recognize as the supreme judge in matters of religion him who has been acknowledged as such by St. Irenaeus, St. Dionysius the Great, St. Athanasius the Great, St. John Chrysostom, St. Cyril, St. Flavian, the Blessed Theodoret, St. Maximus the Confessor, St. Theodore the Studite, St. Ignatius, and so forth—that is to say, the Apostle Peter, who lives in his successors and who did not hear in vain the words of the Lord, "Thou art Peter, and on this rock I will build my Church"—"Strengthen thy brethren"—"Feed my sheep, feed my lambs."

[1] From the French translation published in 1922 by Librarie Stock, Paris, Introduction, p. LXVI.

Chapter XII

THE INFALLIBILITY OF THE POPE

I

THE conversion to Roman Catholicism of Vernon Cecil Johnson (Father Vernon) has evidently unsettled not a few Anglo-Catholics in England. He was a monk of the Society of the Divine Compassion, and one of the most popular mission preachers in the English Church. I heard him give a devotional talk at the London Anglo-Catholic Congress of 1927 in Albert Hall, when he held over ten thousand people in breathless attention for an hour. It was one of the most moving spiritual addresses I have ever heard. He has written a book, *One Lord, One Faith,* which is an explanation of his reasons for submitting to Rome. Its chief merit is its simplicity, and it made upon me a strong emotional impression. I can imagine it must have had a disturbing effect on thousands who have been deeply stirred or converted by his mission preaching, or have been under his spiritual direction.

The book has been answered by two Cambridge scholars, the Rev. Wilfred L. Knox and the Rev. Eric Milner-White, in a little book entitled *One God and Father of All*. In their attempt to refute the claim of Papal Infallibility they go to the other extreme and deny the infallibility of the Church. For this they have been severely criticized by *The Church Times*. Rome and the East have always held that the Catholic Church is an infallible teacher of the faith. That has also been the contention of Anglo-Catholic theologians by whom I have been chiefly influenced in the past. These two somewhat Modernistic Anglo-Catholics apparently subscribe to the statement in the Thirty-Nine Articles that "as the Church of Jerusalem, Alexandria, and Antioch, have erred; so also the Church of Rome hath erred, not only in their living and manner of Ceremonies, but also in matters of faith." It is said to be a strong card in overtures for reunion with the East that Constantinople is not said to have erred, but it is more likely that the framers of the Articles did not recognize Constantinople as a patriarchal see.

If the Catholic Church is not infallible, then the individual Christian is left without any sure and infallible guidance in matters of faith and morals. These two Cambridge writers assert that the belief in the infallibility of the Church stands on the same

level as the belief in the inspiration of Holy Scripture. As they consider that belief in Biblical inspiration is no longer binding on the Catholic conscience,
so they think that the day will come when Catholics
will no longer regard the Church as infallible. They
do not however reject the authority of the Church.
They maintain that the authority of the Catholic
creeds and the decrees of the seven undisputed ecumenical councils is due to the fact that they were
accepted by the undivided Church as being true
statements of what the Church had always believed.
The authority of the Church is as great in its sphere
as the authority of science—greater in fact, since
science has no Christ at its beginning, its middle and
its end; but infallibility cannot be claimed for the
authority of the Church any more than for the
authority of science.

This then is the best argument that two of the
most learned Anglo-Catholics can put up against
Rome, that we can no longer accept the Catholic
Church as an infallible guide in faith and morals,
but are thrown back upon the accepted results of
theological scholarship and the interpretation of
Scripture by the individual. What is this but the
substitution of private judgment for the authority
of the Church, which has always been the foundation
principle of Protestantism?

many cases they presided. The decrees of these general councils were not considered final unless confirmed by the Bishop of Rome. His confirmation made the councils ecumenical.

III

"The early Church recognized that the Pope has the final word in matters of faith, no less than in those of discipline; that she herself is protected by God against heresy. Put that together, and you have, implicitly, what the Vatican Council defined." Thus Adrian Fortescue, in his admirable little book on *The Early Papacy* (p. 14) tersely states the argument for Papal Infallibility.

In every religious and secular organization, there must be a final court of appeal. In the United States we have the Supreme Court. Its decisions are final, and their authority must be accepted by all. We do not regard its decisions as infallible, because God has given no pledge of infallibility to the American nation. If He had, then the decisions of the Supreme Court would necessarily be infallible.

With the Catholic Church it is otherwise. God has promised that His Church would be indefectible and infallible. Her Divine Founder said, "On this rock I will build my Church, and the gates of hell shall not prevail against it." He also said, "When He, the Spirit of Truth, is come, He will guide you into all truth." He promised to be with His apostles—and by implication with their successors—till the end of the world; and He gave them a pledge of His perpetual guidance in their teaching when He said, "He that heareth you heareth me." Therefore it is not going too far to say, in the words of Fortescue, "The Church cannot make a mistake in her own business, because God has given her to us to be our certain guide in religion." (p. 53.)

If then we believe on the authority of our Lord that His Church is infallible, we must also believe that the court of last appeal in the Church is infallible. Historically the See of Peter has been the court of last appeal from the beginning. St. Peter was the court of last appeal in the first Council of Jerusalem. This has seemed to me one of the most obvious facts in the history of the early Church. To explain it away requires more of the ability of a special pleader than I can muster. I have been trying to explain it away for thirty years, and I am now exhausted. When we couple this plain historical fact of the common acknowledgment of the supreme authority of the Roman See in settling controversies of faith, with our Lord's promise to St. Peter, "I will pray for thee that thy faith fail not," we have sufficient justification for believing in Papal Infallibility.

I cannot doubt that this was the faith of the early Church. The affair of the Montanists excommunicated by Pope Zephyrinus, the condemnation of Denis of Alexandria, of Jovinian, and of Euthyches, were all cases in which the Popes made the final decision on questions of faith. I have already shown that St. Irenaeus taught that the Church of Rome has a mightier rule than any other Church, that every Church must agree with her, and that because of this agreement, the true tradition is kept in the other Churches. St. Cyprian of Carthage declares that the See of Peter is the chief Church whence priestly unity has come, and that the African schismatics "had not considered that the Romans are those whose faith is praised by the Apostle, to whom perfidy cannot have access." The historian Sozomen, in describing how Pope Damasus I condemned the heresy which made the Holy Ghost less than God, says: "When this question was discussed and grew from day to day from love of debate, the Bishop of the city Rome, having heard of the matter, wrote to the Churches of the East that they must confess the consubstantial Trinity equal in honor and glory, as do the Western bishops. When he did this all were quiet, as the controversy was ended by the judgment of the Roman Church; and this question at last seemed to be ended." In 416, two synods were held in Africa to deal with the Pelagian heresy, one at Carthage, and one at Mileve. Both submitted their decrees to Pope Innocent I for his confirmation. When the Papal letter arrived at Mileve, St. Augustine made his famous remark: "Already two synods have sent to the apostolic see concerning this affair. The rescripts have come from there; the cause is finished. Would that at last the error were finished too." The Emperor Valentinian III (423–455) wrote: "We must defend the faith handed down by our fathers with all care; and we must keep the proper reverence due to the blessed Apostle Peter incorrupt in our time also. Therefore the most blessed Bishop of the Roman city, to whom ancient right has given the authority of the priesthood over all, shall have his place, and power to judge about the faith and about bishops." Who has not heard of the famous cry that went up from the assembled bishops at the Council of Chalcedon, after the *Tome* of Pope Leo the Great had been read to them: "This is the faith of the fathers; this the faith of the apostles. We all believe so; the orthodox believe so. Anathema to him who does not so believe. Peter has spoken thus through Leo."

I cannot refrain from quoting this stirring passage from Dr. Fortescue's brilliant book:

Chalcedon in 451 brings us to the end of our period. But it does not by any means bring us to the end of texts we could quote. Peter spoke through Leo when Monophysitism threatened the Church. Other storms were to threaten the people of Christ during the centuries that followed Chalcedon. Many times again the waves have threatened to wreck the ship; but always Christ was in her, always the man whom Christ appointed was at her helm. Through sixteen more centuries Peter has spoken through a Leo, a Gregory, an Innocent, a Pius. Living and ruling on his throne by the Tiber, Peter still gives the faith to those who seek it. Today Peter speaks through a Benedict. Benedict will go to his account, as his predecessors have gone to theirs, but the voice of Peter will not die with him. For twenty centuries more, if the world last so long, Peter will live in his successors, and will speak, when need arises, through them; till at the end the last Pope hands back to his Master the heavy burden of those keys that the first received on the shore of the Lake of Galilee.

Chapter XIII

ANGLICAN ORDERS

I

To my mind it seems reasonable that all considerations about validity of orders and jurisdiction should begin with an attempt to ascertain the mind of our Lord Jesus Christ. He is the Good Shepherd, the Pastor who rules over the whole flock which He has redeemed with His Precious Blood. No one may presume to exercise the office of pastor over the flock of Christ on his own initiative or by his own authority. Unless a man be commissioned by the Great Shepherd of the sheep, he is but a usurper. "He that entereth not by the door into the sheepfold, but climbeth up some other way, the same is a thief and a robber."

Nothing can be clearer from the study of the Gospels than that our Saviour gave to St. Peter the chief pastoral charge over His flock. After the Resurrection, on a most solemn occasion, He thrice emphasized the command to St. Peter, "Feed my sheep." This commission must be interpreted as covering not simply the few remaining years of St. Peter's life on earth, but as continuing till the end of the world. All who believe in the ministry of apostolic succession interpret our Lord's words to His apostles, "Lo, I am with you all the days, even unto the end of the world," as a guaranty of His continued presence not only with His apostles but also with their successors throughout all the ages to come. The same interpretation may reasonably be placed on His charge to St. Peter.

Therefore I cannot but feel that if I am to have pastoral charge over any portion of the flock of Christ, I must receive my jurisdiction from the living successor of St. Peter, the Bishop of Rome, or someone commissioned by him with the power of giving jurisdiction. I may then feel assured that I am exercising my ministry with the authority of Jesus Christ. In this connection I have been impressed with those words of Pope Leo XIII at the beginning of his Apostolic Letter, *Apostolicae Curae*, "Helped by His grace, We endeavor to fulfill the office and follow in the footsteps of 'the Great Shepherd of the sheep,' Our Lord Jesus Christ."

This question of jurisdiction is of primary importance in all questions relating to the Christian ministry. It completely overshadows all questions

about the validity of orders. If our Lord intended
that His Church should have an administrative head,
and appointed St. Peter as the first one to hold that
position, then the supreme power of jurisdiction
over the whole flock of Christ is exercised by his
successors in the See of Rome, as they have claimed
from the beginning. The fact that I have not received jurisdiction from a bishop in communion
with the apostolic see is what has troubled me most
during this past year when I have been seriously re-
considering my whole ecclesiastical position. For
even if my orders were valid, as I have assumed all
along on the basis of my spiritual experience and
the authority of Anglo-Catholic scholars, yet I have
no right to exercise my priesthood if I have not received proper jurisdiction. It goes deeper than that.
Leaving out all questions of the right to perform
priestly functions, and accepting only the Protestant conception of the ministry as a pastoral leadership over the souls committed to my care, I have
no right to exercise such leadership without authority from the successor of him whom our Lord
made chief pastor of His flock.

The Good Shepherd laid down His life for the
sheep. His pastors must be animated by the same
spirit of sacrifice. By virtue of their office they are
commissioned to offer the Holy Sacrifice of the

Mass, a true propitiatory sacrifice for the living and the dead. To be in harmony with the Sacrifice which they offer day by day, they must be men who bear the marks of sacrifice in their lives. They must be sacrificing priests in every sense of the word. Moreover, the terms of their ordination should be unambiguous, in intention, form and matter; so that the faithful may know that they have been given authority to offer the Sacrifice of the Body and Blood of Christ, and have received proper jurisdiction.

II

The Catholic Church has received from her Founder the authority to determine what rites and ceremonies shall be used in conferring the sacrament of holy orders. The old Sarum Rite, which had been used in England for many centuries before the Reformation, used perfectly explicit terms which were clearly meant to ordain a sacrificing priesthood. It was definitely stated that the Holy Ghost was given for the office and work of a priest or a bishop. Cranmer changed all this. In the new Ordinal, which he composed for the First Prayer Book of Edward VI, he expunged all reference to a sacrificing priesthood, just as in sixteen different places he eliminated the idea of sacrifice from the Communion Office. He also discontinued the giving of the chalice and paten to the ordinand, and substituted for it the giving of the Bible. It was unmistakably his intention to emphasize preaching and pastoral care as the chief work of the ministry, and to omit all references to the offering of the Holy Sacrifice of the Mass.

Down to the time of the Reformation, in the "form" that was used in every part of the Church, whether East or West, for ordaining men to the priesthood, the office of priesthood was formally expressed. This was true of the Ancient Roman Rite (the Leonine Sacramentary), the Ancient Gallican, the Greek, the Coptic, the Syro-Jacobite, the Maronite, the Nestorian, the Armenian, the Apostolic Constitutions, and the Canons of St. Hippolytus. In every case the words of the "form" are conjoined with the laying on of hands, which latter constitutes the "matter" of the sacrament of holy orders. The same thing was true of the form used for conferring the episcopate.

It remained for Cranmer to make an entirely new departure by omitting all mention of priesthood or episcopate in the "forms" which he composed for the Edwardine Prayer Book, which forms were used in all Anglican ordinations from 1559 to 1662. The Edwardine form for ordaining priests is as follows:

Receive the Holy Ghost; whose sins thou dost for-
give, they are forgiven; and whose sins thou dost retain,
they are retained. And be thou a faithful dispenser of
the Word of God, and of His holy Sacraments: in the
name of the Father, and of the Son, and of the Holy
Ghost. Amen.

The form for consecrating bishops was likewise
simplified beyond all recognition:

Take the Holy Ghost, and remember that thou stir
up the grace of God which is in thee by imposition of
hands: for God hath not given us the spirit of fear, but
of power, and love, and soberness.

The seminary students who are preparing to be
ordained to the ministry of the Episcopal Church
labor under a great disadvantage. As they study the
present Anglican Ordinal, as contained in the
Prayer Book, the Ordinal that has been in use since
1662, they find "forms" quite different from those
imposed on the English Church by Cranmer. The
form for ordaining to the priesthood begins as follows: "Receive the Holy Ghost for the office and
work of a priest in the Church of God, now committed unto thee by the imposition of our hands."
The form for the episcopate is also quite satisfactory from the point of view of Catholic usage:
"Receive the Holy Ghost, for the office and work
of a bishop in the Church of God, now committed

unto thee by the imposition of our hands: in the name of the Father, etc." The average theological student, not knowing much about ordinations, naturally assumes that these forms are sufficient to make priests and bishops in the sense in which these orders have been regarded in the Church from the apostles' time. He is usually not told, or if so the point is not emphasized, that for a hundred years a defective form was used for all ordinations in the English Church. The defects of the Ordinal were made good in the revision of 1662, so far as the "form" was concerned, but this change came too late. In the hundred years that had elapsed, the apostolic succession was lost in the Church of England.

Nor will it do to say that Cranmer's form, in leaving out the conferring of the power to offer the Sacrifice of the Mass, was but a return to the earliest form in use in the Catholic Church, and if that invalidated it, there are no valid ordinations in the Catholic Church. This is the argument of the authors of *One God and Father of All.* It is not necessary for a valid form to contain both the word "priesthood," and the mention of its chief function, consecration or offering; but one *or* the other is essential to a valid rite. Cranmer's form leaves out both, and that is true of no other form in use anywhere in the Catholic Church of the West or the Orthodox East before the Reformation. Moreover the fact that Cranmer did leave out both, and also discontinued the giving of the chalice and paten, is to me convincing evidence of his intention, and the intention of the Church of England, to abolish the priesthood in the traditional Catholic sense of the word.

The First Prayer Book of Edward VI, with its Ordinal, was the joint work of Archbishop Cranmer and Bishop Ridley. The Second Prayer Book, composed under the same auspices, and with further deletions of anything that taught the Catholic doctrine of the Holy Communion or the ministry, was modified only slightly by a committee appointed by Queen Elizabeth on her accession to the throne. This committee was composed of eight men, who were notorious for their heretical views on the sacraments and the ministry: Grindal, Pilkington, Whitehead, Sandys, Cox, Parker, Bell and May. Anyone who wishes to take the time can consult the writings of these men, and satisfy himself as to their doctrinal intentions. I have space only to quote from Cranmer and Ridley.

Archbishop Cranmer, in his treatise on *The Lord's Supper*, Book V, p. 352, writes: "As for saying or singing Mass by the priest, as it was in times past used, it is neither a sacrifice propitiatory nor yet a sacrifice of laud and thanksgiving, nor in any way allowed before God, but abominable and detestable." Ridley, the first Anglican Bishop of London, in 1550 gave orders for the destruction of all the altars in the parish churches of London, and the substitution of tables such are still to be found in many Anglican churches everywhere. He was trying to root out of the minds of people the idea that the Mass was a Sacrifice. On p. 51 of his *Works,* he writes: "They (Catholics) believe that the sacrament was not the sacrament but the thing itself whereof it is a sacrament; that the creature (the consecrated Host) was the Creator, and that the thing which had neither life nor sense was the Lord Himself. . . . Laws are made to maintain that heinous idolatry wherein that adoration is given unto the lifeless and dumb creature (the consecrated Host) which is only due unto the ever-living God. Yea, they say they can and do make of bread both man and God by their transubstantiation. O wicked invention and Satan's own brood!"

III

While the laying on of hands of a bishop, as provided in the Anglican Ordinal of 1552, would satisfy the requirements of the Catholic Church as to the matter of the sacrament of orders, that must be conjoined with the proper form and intention. I am now convinced that the form used for a hundred years until 1662 was defective for the purpose of conferring priest's or bishop's orders; and that the intention of the Reformers was plainly to abolish the priesthood and the episcopate as they have always been understood by the Catholic Church.

As a further indication of this change in intention it is interesting to note what conception of the ministry prevailed in England from 1559 to 1662. If the contention of Anglo-Catholics that the old orders were continued in the reformed Church were true, then we should find plenty of evidence for it in the theological writers of the time. It will not do to rely on the fact that the terms "priest" and "bishop" were retained in the Prayer Book. What's in a name? The question is, what did the terms connote? It was a common assumption in all Elizabethan literature that the English clergy were no longer "Mass-priests." Hooker's *Ecclesiastical Polity* was one of the representative theological works of the time. In Book V, Chap. lxxviii, Sec. 3, he writes as follows:

Seeing then that sacrifice is no part of the Church ministry, how should the name of priesthood be thereunto rightly applied? . . . The Fathers of the Church . . . call usually the ministry of the Gospel priesthood in regard of that which the Gospel hath proportionable to ancient sacrifices, namely, the communion of the Blessed Body and Blood of Christ, although it have properly now no sacrifice. As for the people, when they hear the name, it draweth no more their minds to any cogitation of sacrifice than the name of a senator or an alderman causeth them to think of old age.

I have been treating Anglican orders mainly with reference to priesthood, because I am naturally interested in determining whether my orders are valid; but I cannot pass over lightly the change which was made in the oath which bishops are required to take when they are consecrated. Under the old order they took two oaths at the time of their elevation to the episcopate: a confession of faith, and an oath of allegiance to the Pope as Head of the Church. Both were omitted from Cranmer's Ordinal, and for them was substituted an oath of allegiance to the King as the Supreme Head of the Church. That accounts for many things in the subsequent history of the English Church down to our own time. The bishops are primarily henchmen of the secular power.

The Oxford Movement has made valiant efforts to restore the Catholic conception of the priesthood and the episcopate in the various national Churches of the Anglican Communion. Nevertheless, if a poll were taken today of the clergy of the Anglican Church throughout the world, the vast majority of them would say that they did not believe in the Sacrifice of the Mass or in their right to hear confessions. They do not regard the Anglican Communion Service as the Mass; and whatever their private beliefs may be, they do not act as if they believe in the Real Presence of Christ in the Eucharist. Neither does the Prayer Book Communion Office contain any clear-cut phrases that imply belief in the Mass as a true Sacrifice. It is merely a commemoration of the Sacrifice once offered on the Cross.

Those who maintain that the Anglican Church has a valid priesthood must face consequences not altogether pleasant to contemplate. For, if their opinion holds, it means that vast numbers of her bishops and priests are consecrating the bread and wine in the Holy Communion to be the true Body and Blood of Christ without believing that they are doing so, that they are offering the Sacrifice of the Mass without intending to do so, and that they possess the gift of priestly absolution but

never exercise it. It means also that bishops who
have no intention of ordaining sacrificing priests
can by means of the Anglican ordinal confer a
sacrificing priesthood on men who have no intention of receiving it. To believe that is to believe in
magic, and goes far beyond the wildest accusations
of the Bishop of Birmingham, Dr. Barnes.

What I have said applies to the Cranmer Ordinal,
which was the only ordinal in use in the Church of
England for a hundred years after the Reformation.
But even the present ordinal is so ambiguous as to
make it defective. It is permissible to use the alter-
native form which says nothing about the power of
absolution. This form is as follows: "Take thou
Authority to execute the Office of a Priest in the
Church of God, now committed to thee by the
Imposition of our hands. And be thou a faithful
Dispenser of the Word of God, and of his holy
Sacraments." Thus the intention of the Church is
not clear. As in so many other matters, no man can
say what is the official teaching of the Anglican
Church.

I am driven to the conclusion that the Papal
contention that at the Reformation the Anglican
Church intentionally departed from the historic
Catholic conception of the ministry is borne out

by the facts. St. Thomas Aquinas said in his *Summa
Theologica* (III, qu. 60, Art. 8) : "It is clear that if
any substantial part of the sacramental form be
suppressed, the essential sense of the words is destroyed, and consequently the sacrament becomes
invalid." I feel therefore that I am compelled to
accept as true the judgment of Pope Leo XIII in
his Bull on Anglican Orders:

The words which even up to the present time have
been considered, speaking generally, by Anglicans as the
form proper to the ordination of a priest, namely, "Receive the Holy Ghost," signify very indefinitely the order of priesthood, or the grace and power of it, which
especially is the power of consecrating and offering the
true Body and Blood of the Lord. . . . In the matter
of episcopal consecration, the case is similar . . .
with this fundamental lack of form is joined a defect
of intention. . . . If a rite be changed with the manifest intention, so that another, not received by the
Church, may be introduced, and so that that which the
Church does may be rejected, and which from its institution pertains to the nature of the sacrament, then,
obviously, not only is the intention necessary to the
sacrament lacking, but more, there is an intention opposed to and repugnant to the sacrament. . . . And
so, agreeing with the decrees of all the preceding Pon-
tiffs in this very matter, and confirming them fully,
and so to say, renewing them, by Our authority, of Our

own accord, with certain knowledge, We pronounce
and declare that ordinations according to the Anglican
rite have been acts wholly invalid and that they are
completely null.

Causa finita est! I cannot believe that Rome will
ever reopen the question. Consequently I feel that
those who are working and hoping for corporate
reunion are chasing rainbows. The only path to
reunion is through individual submission.

I hear many of my friends saying: "How can you
deny the spiritual experiences of all these years?
Have you never received Christ at the altars of the
Church? Have you never had your sins forgiven,
or conveyed forgiveness to others in the sacrament
of penance? Has your whole ministry been without
spiritual fruit?" In answer I would say that I believe all my spiritual experiences have been real,
and that the work for souls that God has performed
through my ministry has been real.

Let me prove this statement by quoting from a
Catholic writer of unimpeachable orthodoxy,
Father Woodlock, S.J. In his valuable and (for
Anglicans) very upsetting little book on *Constanti-
nople, Canterbury and Rome* (p. 57) he says:

This is a "hard saying"; perhaps the greatest
stumbling block in the path of clergymen who otherwise would submit to the Pope and enter the Catholic

fold. They feel that to submit would be to deny the spiritual experiences of their priestly life; they cannot deny the evident fact that when they received Communion or celebrated they *felt* Christ had come to them and the fruit of the Holy Spirit was produced in their souls.

They need not deny a single one of these experiences. Bishop Gore says that he "must acknowledge the same reality of the fruits of the Spirit in the Society of Friends (the Quakers) which ignores baptism." Catholic theology and devotion recognize that what is called a "spiritual communion," without the Real Presence of Christ under the sacramental species, may be the means of receiving, on occasions, greater graces than are received when Christ is bodily present at a sacramental communion. "God is not tied to His own ordinances," as Dr. Gore declares; and men who believe sincerely in the priesthood of the English Church ministers, may receive an outpouring of grace in their ministrations which to them is subjectively indistinguishable from strictly sacramental graces.

Their Church may be—and is—without the abiding Presence of our Eucharistic Lord; the Sacrament they have to fight so hard to reserve may be—and is—but a wafer of flour and water; but their love and devotion, their prayers and fastings, their zeal to make God's House beautiful, and their ceremonies seemly—all these things witness to hearts that are hungry for the Bread of Heaven, and God has made up to them, we hope and trust, for that of which Cranmer deprived them in his protestant, fanatical hatred of the Sacrifice of the Mass.

Is this line of argument a justification for remaining in the Anglican Church? If in spite of the invalidity of Anglican orders the faithful members of the Anglican Church receive an outpouring of grace through their Church's ministrations which is subjectively indistinguishable from strictly sacramental grace, why should they submit to the Pope? It all depends on whether they can continue as Anglicans in good faith, that is whether they still believe that the Anglican Church is really part of the Catholic Church, possessing a valid priesthood and episcopate. If one ceases to believe that, he can no longer remain in good faith. So long as he is blind to the defects of the Anglican system, he is in good faith. When once he sees, then it would be sin for him to remain. This is the principle laid down by our Lord when He declared: "For judgment I am come into this world, that they which see not might see; and that they which see might be made blind." To the humble-minded He gives the gift of faith; to the intellectually proud, spiritual blindness.

EPILOGUE

It is characteristic of my type of mind that I postpone decisions as long as possible, and avoid making investigations the result of which is likely to be upsetting. I must confess that I had never read Pope Leo XIII's Bull which declared Anglican orders invalid until I began working on this chapter. Long ago I read the reply to the Bull made by the Anglican archbishops, together with many other defenses of Anglican orders. I wish now I had read the Bull, *Apostolicae Curae*, thirty years ago. It might have made a vast difference in my subsequent life.

At the time when I began writing this book, I made a resolution that I would make no change in my ecclesiastical position until I had completed my argument. I can always work things out better in writing than by abstract reasoning. In writing I can proceed step by step, as in climbing a mountain. To a mountain climber the whole ascent looks impossible from the valley. But one can always take the next step, and with every step there is that much gained. Because of my dislike of hurting those who had trusted me, I wanted to remain where I was as long as I could do so conscientiously. If only the customary Anglican arguments against Rome might continue to appeal to me, I would hold my ground, even though disillusioned and disheartened.

One by one these arguments have broken in my hands. I came to see that St. Peter had undeniably been given by our Lord the position of supremacy in the apostolic college. As I read over once more the history of the early Church I became convinced that the Petrine tradition was carried on by the Bishops of Rome, and that on this ground their supremacy was everywhere recognized. I discovered that the Church in Rome from the very beginning became the regulative norm for the whole Church, in doctrine, in discipline, in the orders of the ministry, and in the formation of the Canon of Scripture. I learned that the general councils became ecumenical only when confirmed by the Bishop of Rome. I had to admit that the infallibility of the Catholic Church necessarily carried with it the infallibility of her chief Bishop. Finally, I was driven to the conclusion that for one hundred years after the Reformation no valid orders were conferred in the Church of England, and that therefore she lost the apostolic succession. That meant that I was not a priest, and never had been.

After coming to such a conclusion, there was only one course open for me. Immediately after the close of the Diocesan Convention, I called upon Father Ford, the Catholic Chaplain of Columbia University, and told him of my decision. Through his kind offices an interview was arranged with Cardinal Hayes. His Eminence received me most graciously, and after listening patiently to my story, told me the steps that I should take. I then resigned from my parish, wrote to Bishop Manning renouncing the ministry of the Protestant Episcopal Church, and left for a ten-day retreat in the Benedictine Priory at Portsmouth, R. I. There my old friend, Father Sargent (now Dom Leonard), gave me instructions preparatory to my reception into the Catholic Church. I was received by Monsignor McMahon in the Church of Our Lady of Lourdes, on the Feast of St. John the Baptist.

APPENDIX

BOOKS THAT HAVE HELPED ME

CATHOLIC

Catholicisme et Papauté, by Pierre Batiffol. Gabalda, Paris, 1925.

Constantinople, Canterbury and Rome. F. Woodlock, S.J. Longmans, 1923.

Eglises Séparées, by Mgr. Duchesne.

Early History of the Christian Church. 3 Vols. by Mgr. Duchesne. Longmans, 1915.

The Early Papacy, by Adrian Fortescu. Burns, Oates & Washbourne, 1920.

Essay on the Development of Christian Doctrine, by Cardinal Newman.

Apologia pro Vita Sua, by Cardinal Newman.

Life of Cardinal Newman, by J. Lewis May. The Dial Press, 1930.

One Lord, One Faith, by Vernon Cecil Johnson. Longmans, 1929.

Dropping the Hyphen, by Sheila Kaye-Smith. *Dublin Review*, January, 1930.

The Spirit of Catholicism, by Karl Adam. The Macmillan Co. 1929.

NON-CATHOLIC

Le Quatrième Evangile, by Alfred Loisy. Published by the Author.

History of Dogma, by Adolf Harnack.

The See of Peter, by Shotwell and Loomis. Columbia University Press, 1927.

The Eastern Churches and the Papacy, by Rev. S. Herbert Scott. Sheed and Ward, 1928.

Address on Reunion, by Lord Halifax.

St. Peter and St. Paul in the New Testament and in the Early Church, by Professor C. H. Turner in *Theology*. Aug. and Oct., 1926.

Authority in the Church, by Canon T. A. Lacey. Morehouse Publishing Co., Milwaukee, 1928.

One God and Father of All, by Eric Milner-White and Wilfred L. Knox. Morehouse Publishing Co., Milwaukee, 1929.

Peter, Prince of the Apostles, by Professor F. H. Foakes Jackson. Doran, 1927.

La Russie et l'Eglise Universelle, by V. Soloviev. 4th Edition. Stock, Paris, 1922.

The Christian Ecclesia, by Dr. F. J. Hort.